"The 'you gotta do it' book from Burrel I've been waiting for!"
— **Baron Davis: NBA Star**

"Clear, sensible, actionable and inspiring..."
— **Cade McNown: NFL Star and Businessman**

"Burrel's a for-real player who knows what it takes to win."
— **Zach Randolph: NBA Star**

Burrel

www.steetwisespeaking.com

Photography & Design by David M. Pruter
david@pruter.com | www.davidpruter.com

Burrel's wardrobe supplied by
Morris & Sons | www.morrisandsons.com

SUCCESS FOR LIFE

7 STREETWISE STRATEGIES GUARANTEED TO TRANSFORM YOU FROM *WANNABLE* TO *WINNER!*

BURREL LEE WILKS III

"Because Success Requires No Explanation and Failure Allows No Alibi!"

For information:
Burrel Streetwise Inc.
308 East 38th Street
Suite 17A
New York, New York 10016

ISBN-10: 0976873613
ISBN-13: 9780976873617
Library of Congress Control Number: 2007906457

Interior Design and Editorial Services:
The Roberts Group, www.editorialservice.com
Additional Editorial Services:
Heather Anderson, bossofmemedia@gmail.com
Cover Design and Photography: David Pruter, David@Pruter.com
Distribution: Independent Publishers Group, www.IPGbook.com

CONTENTS

CLARENCE JONES:
Civil Rights Leader and Legal Advisor
to Dr. Martin Luther King Jr.

I met Burrel Lee Wilks III a few years ago while on a visit to L.A. and was immediately struck by the combination of charisma, certainty, and realism represented by this likeable, young black man who'd come through the streets to become a successful businessman and sought-after life coach.

Fresh, confident voices and empowering leadership are required today more than ever, as the intense demands of a material, media-driven world compel us to look for shortcuts, or as Burrel suggests, to chase "moments of satisfaction" often at the expense of real, sustainable personal success.

And that's exactly where Burrel comes in. This "streetwise graduate of life" keeps it real, honest, and authentic as he translates his life experiences into the kind of practical, road-tested lessons of "success for life" that each and every one of us can activate. Burrel contends that there are three pillars to success: a reliable internal navigation system, people-power, and, ultimately, the ability to tap into your own bottomless resources of self-confidence, ingenuity, and individuality. You certainly won't find me arguing with any of that. Burrel Lee Wilks is after all, a Streetwise MBA: a Master of Being Alive.

ACKNOWLEDGMENT

With love and appreciation to Janet, my wife and coauthor (we make a great team!) and to both our families. Special thanks too, to those friends and colleagues who helped drag this boat through the sand. Much appreciation to Clarence, Elton, Box, Shaquille, Baron and Zach, Cade, Black D., and Trey, and a heartfelt shout out to Messiah: you're a big part of the story, bro. Stay strong.

Success requires no explanation.
Failure allows no alibi.

I grew up in the 'hood. The real 'hood . . . the kind most people only see in movies. We lived in Chicago, where my dad was a city sanitation worker and my mom worked as a secretary. You're probably picturing what everybody else saw from the outside: just another stereotypical inner-city black family, struggling to make ends meet.

Except, truth was, my dad had another job. His own business, actually. By day, he was a lowly, unassuming garbage man. But by night, my old man was a big-time kingpin, bringing in drugs by the truckload, and bills by the tens of thousands.

For real.

Being the oldest son, I did what many American men have done throughout our history: I took over the family business.

Believe it or not, being a gang chief isn't so different from being the CEO of a corporation. Hundreds of employees under my leadership operated a number of profitable businesses. I had the kind of responsibilities any Fortune 500 executive might: supply, distribution, sales, accounting and payroll, recruiting, employee retention, and motivation.

Ultimately, I came to realize that though my leadership qualifications may not have come from Harvard or Wharton, they came from the best school of all. Naturally enough, most people underestimate the power of the "university of the streets," but the skills I used to build a business empire, close million-dollar deals, keep egos in check, negotiate turf, and frankly, stay alive, are simply basic fundamentals of a results-oriented and timeless human behavior system.

In the end, success on the streets, and anywhere else for that matter, largely depends on how well we understand and manage "people relationships." Whether you want to take over Madison Avenue or the street corner; win on the basketball court or in the classroom—

to achieve sustainable success, you must first become a master of "people power"—starting with yourself.

In the end, that's what these Streetwise Strategies are all about: showing you how, by harnessing the force of your personality, positive energy, smarts, and influence, and applying certain principles to how you live, you can unlock limitless stores of power and potential.

Success requires no explanation, and failure allows no alibi. Are you a player or a wannabe? Only you can decide. But let me promise you this: once you apply these seven Streetwise Strategies to your life, there will be no stopping you.

I will never have a heart attack. I give them.
George Steinbrenner
Businessman and Owner of the New York Yankees

SUCCESS

Part 1

Wannabe or Winner: Ready to Play to Win?

What, ultimately, makes the difference between leaders and losers, achievers and strivers, winners and wannabes?

1

SUCCESS:
A UNIVERSAL GOAL?

*There's a fine line
between fishing and just standing
on the shore like an idiot.*

Steven Wright,
<u>**Comedian**</u>

SUCCESS FOR LIFE

*I have the same goal I've had ever since I was a girl.
I want to rule the world.*

**Madonna,
Entertainer**

Everyone wants his or her life to be a slice of something rich and wonderful. Doesn't matter if your dream is to be famous and make millions or retire into obscurity; if you want to see your kids through college or see the sunrise from the top of Mount Kilimanjaro; or if you simply want to live life with confidence, love, and security: we're each seeking some kind of success.

Success may be defined differently for each of us. Does your success hinge on wealth, health, happiness, security, or love? For the majority of us, it's a blend of all these things, but whichever way you come at it, the drive for success is a goal we all have in common.

So, you may say, "Burrel, show me the shortcuts, man!" True, I've taken a few of those in my life, but I'm gonna put it to you straight: when it comes to success, there are no shortcuts. The only true magic is the stuff you pull from inside yourself, and the only direct route to success for life is to get rid of your negative behaviors and replace them with positive ones you'll stick with for life. Once you learn how to pull this power from inside and channel it positively, you generate something I call *life-velocity*. Once you've got that unstoppable forward momentum, the seemingly impossible becomes probable!

- So, no, you can't choose your birthright, but you can choose the way you live.

- You didn't have a say in your genetic heritage, but you can sculpt your mind and body into the best shape they can be.

- You can't change the whole world, but you can change *your* world.

- You can't recapture your youth, but you can stay young in mind and spirit.

- You may only be five-foot nothing, but you can still be a Giant.

- You can never be eighteen again, but you can reinvent and rejuvenate yourself.

- You probably won't win the lottery, but you can grow rich in many other ways.

The fact is, there're lots more things we CAN achieve than not. It's as simple as this: If your thinking is *limited*, then your *life* will be limited, too. Guaranteed. The good news? Well, with a little practice and a lot of focus, we can all *reprogram* ourselves to win.

Champions aren't made in gyms.
Champions are made from something they have deep
inside them—a desire, a dream, a vision.
They have to have last-minute stamina;
they have to be a little faster;
they have to have the skill and the will.
But the will must be stronger than the skill.

Muhammad Ali,
Boxing Heavyweight Champion of the World

So why do so many people fail to achieve sustainable success? Why do so many folks feel more like wannabes than winners, scrabblin' rather than celebratin'? For most people, success proves to be as slippery as a catfish, and though they keep fishin' and grabbin', they never quite manage to land it! Well, stick with me, and I'll show you not only how to catch fish for life, but how to cook 'em, too!

Success is never final. Failure is never fatal.
Courage is what counts.

Sir Winston Churchill,
Prime Minister of England

THREE ESSENTIAL PILLARS OF SUCCESS

Life is either a daring adventure or nothing.

Helen Keller,
Author

Ever see those enormous skyscrapers in New York, Dallas, Chicago, or even Hong Kong? The ones that are perched—almost impossibly it seems—on concrete stilts like a bruiser running back with matchstick legs. They tower over the world below, story upon story; floor after floor; incalculable tons of concrete, steel, glass, and people, apparently defying gravity as they poke through the clouds. I've been a property developer for years, and yet, these extraordinary feats of art and engineering still stop me in my tracks. How could it be possible that such colossal physical masses could be propped up by a few skinny pillars?

Of course, the answer is not in what you see but what you *don't see*. Those pillars are actually concrete and steel tentacles that reach down and up and are so deeply enmeshed with the body of the structure that they become intrinsically and organically part of the building itself. The building isn't propped-up by these pillars—it's built around them. They have become one and the same.

So it is with successful people.

I've spent many years studying success in all its manifestations. From billionaires to ball players, gang chiefs to businessmen, entrepreneurs to entertainers, I've seen success play out in a thousand different guises. And I will simply say this: as many men and women as I've seen achieve success, I've seen many, many more let it slip away from them.

You see, like those skyscrapers soaring into greatness, success can only be built on rock-solid foundations. Then, as it grows and blossoms, it will be stabilized by its own support pillars—pillars built of powerful and positive beliefs, behaviors, and attitudes. And like the supporting structure of any great edifice, these props—your beliefs—must be so deeply rooted in the heart of the construction that they become part of the fabric of the building—part of the fabric of YOU.

> *A successful man is one who can lay a firm foundation with the bricks that others throw at him.*
> **Sidney Greenberg,**
> **Author**

After years of studying success, and the people who've achieved it, I have identified *three essential success pillars* sturdy enough to support a skyscraper and brawny enough to hold it firm through any earthquake or thunderstorm that may come its way.

1. **A Core Navigation System:** You wouldn't set off on a cross-country road trip without a destination in mind, and a map or GPS navigation system in the car, would you? Too darn easy to get lost and what a waste of time, effort, and expense that is. So when it comes to negotiating that most mysterious journey of all—your pathway through life—it stands to reason that you should have a clear end-game in mind, an easily understandable set of directions, and non-negotiable "rules of the road" to keep you firmly on track.

2. **People-power:** Somehow in the noise and pressure of life, it's easy to forget one of the most fundamental principles of success: It's all about the *people*, stupid! Personal success is highly influenced by our ability to effectively engage with—and sway—the people around us. In other words managing human relationships to our best advantage (including the relationship we have with ourself!). This ability to channel people-power is the skill that ultimately sets you apart from the rest of the field. People-savviness is at the very core of Streetwise philosophy and is integrated into all my strategies.

3. **Dogged Self-Belief and Determination:** This is all about what happens on the inside, not the outside. Self-belief is the energy source—the fuel, if you like—that propels us into the stratosphere of success; or, if we don't have it, leaves us sputtering in the mud of failure. Focus guarantees we're propelled in the right direction. Determination keeps the engine turning over even when it feels as though we're running on empty! Many successful people rank perseverance as their single most critical success-quality.

These, then, are the ingredients—the foundations—of a successful life. We'll be looking at exactly what it takes to build these three critical success pillars throughout this book, and though it's useful to read the sections sequentially, it's also fine to dip in and dip out at any point that grabs your attention. There's a ton of practical advice, real-life stories, tip lists, and motivation between these covers—enjoy, and hopefully you'll be joining me soon at The Success Club!*

---

* Burrel Streetwise Online Coaching Club (www.the-success-club.com).

2

WHAT DOES IT MEAN TO BE STREETWISE?

Burrel was unique. You know, there are guys who need to run with the crowd. They draw their energy from it. Well, Burrel was different. It was like, he was electric, like he was his own energy source.

Kevin Rice
Friend

I've been a practicing life coach for most of my forty years. In fact, for just about as many years as I can remember, guys have come to my round-table to sit, talk, and gain a fresh perspective on their lives and problems.

'Course no one called it "life coaching" back then, and you sure as heck couldn't have made a living out of it. In fact, even today guys from the 'hood find it a stretch to believe that anyone would pay to hear someone else talk! After all, talk is free, isn't it?

Well, free or not, it sure didn't stop them from troopin' to my door back then to soak up those priceless words.

Ever since I was a shorty, my phone has rung off the hook, night and day (it still drives my wife crazy), with guys reachin' out. Over the years, I've spun enough words of advice and encouragement to string a silk ladder all the way to the moon—a ladder that more than a few guys are steadily climbing, even today, one rung at a time.

The men who took a seat at my table were often much older than I was, old enough in some cases to be someone's father or even grandfather. Pulling up a chair, they'd light up a smoke, take a puff or two, and then move right to the business at hand. Could I help them resolve a sensitive, political, business, or personal issue? Could I offer them an answer, a solution, or an escape route? Backed into this corner or that corner, uncertain which way to turn, they couldn't see a way out, and their lives were falling apart. Money was owed, jobs lost, businesses failin', wives cheatin' or leavin', kids uncontrollable—the list of woes was endless.

There was Eric, in debt up to his eyeballs and stuck in the trap of having to borrow more to keep afloat. Rodney seemed to start (and close) a new business every week; James was always embroiled in some dispute or turf battle; T. had lost his job—again. And then, of course, there was the endless litany of relationship problems with wives, girlfriends, mistresses, and children.

My counseling responsibilities were never taken lightly. You see in the world we inhabited—Chicago's notoriously tough West Side— the stakes were pretty darn high. Retribution was a harsh reality for those who screwed up, including the very real possibility of finding yourself on the way to an early grave or the penitentiary.

WANNABE OR WINNER?

Use your mentality.
Wake up to reality.

Cole Porter,
Songwriter and Composer

There wasn't an issue that didn't find its way to my round-table. I mediated agreements for all kinds of complex problems. Solutions were created where none had seemed viable. I've calmed heated tempers, soothed hurt prides, injected a jolt of hard reality when required, and talked guys down from the emotional window-ledges on which they teetered.

My secret? Well, I showed them different ways to frame their problem; provided different lenses through which to view the facts. I helped them find new angles, which in turn pointed to fresh responses they may not have considered, and solutions they may not have imagined. The doors of their minds opened to let in enough light to navigate their way to a better place. I gave them helpful tools, too, in the form of insight, confidence, and alternative behaviors. Clarifying, interpreting, advising, and sometimes just plain kickin' ass, I became known as the neighborhood go-to guy when you found yourself in a bind.

It surprised me sometimes how difficult it was for some of these guys to see the way through their predicament, and how *wishy-washy* they could be when it came to making tough choices! You see, for me, more often than not, the solution was crystal clear. Sure, it might require that hard decisions be made and extra effort applied; sometimes it demanded that emotions be suppressed, personal satisfaction be put on the back burner, and a bit of hurt be pocketed. Still, to me, these short-term costs were a relatively small price to pay for the long-term return of getting a life back on track.

Some guys would grab at the diamonds of wisdom I dangled in front of them and fix things. Others wore bad-habit blinders, and that prevented them from seeing their way clear to changing old patterns. For yet others, emotion got in the way, clouding their judgment and leaving them unable to separate the small stuff from the big picture.

11

Then there were the guys who got tripped up on pride or sidetracked by ego. They didn't know how to finesse a solution or find a compromise. They believed anything, other than a head-on confrontation, would be seen as weakness. These were the guys who would never break out of their personal prisons because, for them, *flexibility equaled failure.* They never could understand that the best way to move to the right was sometimes to *feint* to the left.

As the years went by, and the seats at my round-table filled with businessmen, corporate executives, entertainers, sports stars, and even some of Hollywood's elite, it became clear that the issues they each faced were remarkably similar to the ones I'd solved in the streets.

> *The human condition—whether ghetto, corporate*
> *America, or Hollywood hills—is surprisingly*
> *consistent, and whatever situation you find yourself*
> *in, always remember that, under the skin,*
> *the guy across the table is just like you.*
> **Burrel**

Heroic battles are enacted every single day [in the ghetto], as kids struggle to do the right thing. They want to break away all right; they just *don't know how.*

I want to show them that anything is possible, that they can't allow their birthright to define them or conditioning to constrain them. I want to show them that they are building their own jails, from the inside out, but though they've put themselves in lockup, they already have the combination to get out. I want to help them step out into the sunlight.—From *Tattoos on My Soul*

THE REAL LESSONS I LEARNED AT SCHOOL

I probably shouldn't say this,
but I was not much of a book person.
I loved to learn, but I learn by doing.
I learn from my experiences.

Mike Krzyzewski,
Duke University Basketball Coach

Imagine you have the ability to read others people's minds. Perhaps you're dating, and you know exactly what she thinks about you; or maybe you're interviewing for a new job, and you can actually hear the interviewer's thoughts and even predict what salary he plans on offering. Seem like a stretch? Possibly. But *being Streetwise* means learning to read people and situations as easily as you read books.

I baled out of school in the tenth grade, and during the short period I "graced" the classroom with my presence, I was an unholy terror. It's not something I'm proud of—but it's a part of who I am. Anyway, there I was, a precocious, skinny, cocky kid, both bully and businessman, extorting the other pupils, teachers, and even the principal. Bustling, hustling, and gambling my way through lunch hours, and after hours, I made more pocket money than most kids—or grown men—would see in a decade or two. At eleven years old, I had girls on my arm, money in my pocket, and power beyond my years.

I have never let schooling interfere with my education.

Mark Twain,
Author and Humorist

Though I spent more time pursuing business interests than academic achievement, the value of the knowledge I soaked up during these streetwise semesters was incalculable. I may not have learned much about the lives of American presidents, nor the finer points of algebra or grammar, but I learned something even more powerful: I leaned how to read people.

Yup, I learned to read people better than books. Looking into a face, it would take me only a split second to understand the history written there, and no matter what someone's lips might be saying, I could always see their real intention reflected, clear as day, in their eyes. In fact, I became multilingual: able to translate body language as precisely as a second language, and see behavior patterns as sharply as if looking at a picture book. You see, to graduate from the streets with my Streetwise MBA, I had to master human nature, too.

As I navigated my way through the minefield that was my world, I became a master strategist with an intuitive understanding of the power of politics and the politics of power. I developed a finely honed ability to understand the subtext of any situation. I learned how to effectively manage and manipulate "people dynamics" in a positive way—to get the results I wanted, the same way that powerful corporate players do in boardrooms around the world every day.

Not bad for an uneducated kid, eh?

Life, business, power, and leadership, I studied them all. These life skills became weapons in my personal armory, and as I rose through the hierarchy of the streets to became an increasingly influential leader, I learned to apply them with ever-greater precision and escalating effect. You see, a leader on the streets is little different from a leader in the corporate world. Both have to align, inspire, and manage; reward; lead by example; demonstrate drive and commitment; and be resilient, flexible, and capable of consistently outsmarting and outflanking the competition.

Unwittingly, my leadership style as a gang chief emulated that of some of the most successful executives in the corporate world. I built a tight, well-organized team with an "executive steering" committee and empowered "managers."

I mobilized, motivated, disciplined, and rewarded based on clearly defined codes of behavior. I played straight and tough, but fair, and like all the best managers, I grew as I went along. I kept my eyes and mind open, and although I could talk up a storm, I also knew when to listen and learn. I understood at a deep level, that the real root of power lay not in ego-soaked individualism, but in the ability to bring together multiple, self-interested groups, and put together a winning team.

Mind Jedi

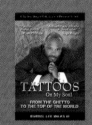

My father may have been infamous for his volatile temper and sometimes violent outbursts, but paradoxically, he also cultivated the art of quiet leadership. The complex choreography of human interaction fascinated me, and I studied diligently.

By scrutinizing group dynamics and body language, I learned to read a meeting's subtext. I watched and listened intently, staying awake into the small hours, eyes darting everywhere. During these long sessions, I honed my ability to read a person's character, and intentions, in a split second: a skill of the highest value in a world where misjudgment could result in a killing or incarceration.—From *Tattoos on My Soul*

3

PLAYING TO WIN: HIGH-STAKES GAME

*If life doesn't offer
a game worth playing,
then invent a new one.*

Anthony J. D'Angelo
Author

SUCCESS FOR LIFE

You win some; you lose some; you wreck some.

**Dale Earnhardt,
NASCAR Legend**

As you can imagine, danger lurked around every corner in my 'hood. Didn't matter whether you were the quietest guy in the world or the wildest; fact is someone, somewhere, had his eye on you. In my world, you were either the user or the used, the top dog or the underdog, the wannabe or the winner.

No, didn't matter whether you were good, bad, or somewhere in-between. Mouse or loudmouth, trouble would soon sniff you out, forcing you to stand up and be counted.

Invisibility was never an option.

And that's the hard, cold truth for us all.

In the end, it makes little difference where you spend your days—street corner or classroom, trading floor or factory floor—it's a dog-eat-dog world out there. There's *always* gonna be a pecking order, with guys climbing on top of the ones below in their hurry to scramble up the ladder, and, on reaching the top rung, doing everything and anything they can to hang on to what they have.

Bet you've had your fingers stomped on more than once.

It might not be obvious now, but pay a little more attention to the dynamics of your home, social scene, and business life. You'll soon see who's pulling the strings and who's hopping around.

I suggest you figure out whether you want to be *the puppet* or *the puppet master.*

Understandably, a lot of people find the idea of being competitive scary, barbaric—dirty even. Distancing themselves from the power-playing, they try to be only about their own business. Problem is, it's tough to mind your own business when everybody else is minding it for you.

So, how can you quit a game when you're already out there on the court and it's not even half-time? There you are, right under the basket, the ball hurtling toward you at full speed. You'd better jump for it and take your best shot, or you're likely to wind up captain of Team Loser.

No. Invisibility is never an option. You can duck when that ball flies at you; keep your head down, your mouth shut; and try to slide on through neutral like Switzerland, but you're only foolin' yourself. No one can hide. *Winners* understand that they're already on the team, on a floodlit court in the thick of the game. They understand that if they *ain't playin'*, they *ain't winnin'*—simple as that.

I'm scared every time I go into the ring,
but it's how you handle it.
What you have to do is plant your feet, bite down
on your mouthpiece, and say,
"Let's go!"

Mike Tyson,
Boxing Heavyweight Champion of the World

IS IT EVER TOO LATE TO WIN?

Life would be infinitely happier
if we could only be born at the age of eighty and
gradually approach eighteen.

Mark Twain,
Author and Humorist

No, it's never too late.

You can't undo, unwind, erase, or "unhappen" steps already taken, words spoken, or decisions made. Shedding one skin and growing a new one ain't gonna fool anyone (least of all you) into thinking you're a brand new person. But the wonderful truth is that we're all living works of art, and because we're living, we're also *growing*.

Look at me. I'm a walking testament to the reality of transformation. I consider myself to be a work in progress (just getting warmed up!), and I have to admit I've had a rocky start. But though I foolishly passed up the colossal gift of a formal education, I still absorbed some of my most profound and enduring life lessons during my formative years.

Do you remember those paint-by-number kits that were popular in the '70s? Well, I was addicted to 'em. By following the instructions and applying paint to the numbered spaces, a fabulous picture—a masterpiece to me, at the ripe old age of seven—would emerge from what had only a few minutes before seemed to be little more than chicken-scratchings.

It was easy, too, even for an attention-challenged bundle of energy and impatience like me. Number 2 was green; 3, blue; 4, a nice sunshine yellow; and 6, my favorite, Ferrari red. And there you had it: a work of art only a mother could love!

But painting by numbers soon became boring:

● Too neat.

● Too constrained.

● Too predictable.

Life, thank goodness, is none of those things.

There's nothing predictable about any aspect of our lives. Our individual portraits are made up of layers of paint, color-on-color, multiple brush strokes and textures. Like impressionist paintings, made up of thousands, even millions, of color pixels, our pictures may seem clearer when viewed from a distance—losing focus and form when we get too close.

> *Life is a great big canvas, and you should throw all the paint on it you can.*
>
> **Danny Kaye,**
> **Actor and Comedian**

We each "paint" our own stories through a mix of experience, experimentation, and trial and error. Each day we add fresh detail, new layers and colors, and an increasingly complex and expressive picture emerges. But we never know what the end result will be. There's no nice photo on the lid of *our* box or instructions telling us which color goes where. Nothing guarantees what the finished product will look like . . .

That's called living.

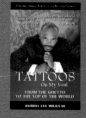

When I look back on my relationship with Tony (Accardo), I realize that he took up where my dad left off. Here I was again at the knee of a giant. My dad had started with a blank canvas on which to paint his mirror image, but Tony took on the much tougher task of scraping off some of the old paint and fashioning a fresh portrait.
—From *Tattoos on My Soul*

Sometimes we arrive at a point when our portrait feels close to being finished, when what we see in the mirror looks and feels right. Ever had those times when you really like where you are in life? When the face looking back at you in the mirror isn't frowning or worried, but happy and content? I hope so, because when you can look in the mirror and your reflection smiles back with satisfaction at what you've achieved and the place you've carved out in this world, well, that's a special moment.

Unfortunately, we can't freeze-frame life just because we happen to like the look of it today. Clocks continue ticking, and some hand bigger than ours keeps slapping new layers of paint onto our portrait—whether we like it or not.

The point is, we never get to see ourselves finished. *We're all works in progress*—not what we were yesterday and not what we'll be tomorrow. And thank goodness for that! It means that no matter what stage you're at—whether you're twenty-one or eighty-one years old; single or married for the fifth time; gang chief, businessman, student, or retiree—your canvas is still propped up on the easel, with time yet to turn it into a masterpiece. No, it's never too late—or too early for that matter—to transform yourself into a force to be reckoned with!

> *It's never too late to be who you might have been.*
> **George Elliot,**
> **Author**

Mine is a rare, celebratory story of transformation. If you're looking for an overnight conversion, a phoenix rising from the ashes, then I'm not your guy. I wasn't a bad kid who one morning woke up a good man. Real life is far messier and more complicated than that. There was no blinding epiphany for me, no sudden moment of stunning clarity. Transforming Burrel Junior, the audacious child-chief who was running his own gang by the age of eleven, into the man I am today took determination, commitment, faith, tenacity, and time. From gangster to life coach and from foolish boy to wise man, my growth was progressive: evolution rather than reinvention. The man I am today is the sum of hundreds, even millions, of choices made, as I forged my own, unique path through life.—From *Tattoos on My Soul*

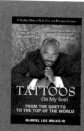

Savvy 7

LATE BLOOMERS

Think you're too old to repaint that picture? It's never too late—these Savvy 7 achievers didn't get started until late in life.

1 After failing at comedy in his twenties, Rodney Dangerfield gave show business another try in his forties, working an office job by day and doing stand-up at night. After years of hard work, he finally got his biggest break at the age of fifty-nine, starring as Al Czenik, a rich obnoxious golfer in the 1980 classic comedy *Caddyshack*.[1]

2 Harlan "Colonel" Sanders was already forty years old when he began cooking chicken for customers at his service station in Corbin, Kentucky. He took another nine years to perfect his secret seasoning blend and build up a reputation across the Bluegrass State. He didn't open his first franchise until the age of sixty-two, but by age seventy-four, Sanders's chicken was being sold at more than six hundred locations nationwide.[2]

3 Laura Ingalls Wilder, author of the *Little House on the Prairie* series, didn't begin writing until she took a position as a columnist in her forties. She didn't publish her first book, *Little House in the Big Woods*, until age sixty-five.[3]

4 Famous American painter Anna Mary "Grandma" Moses didn't even start painting until she was in her seventies; in fact, she took up painting only after arthritis forced her to quit her first love, embroidery. It wasn't until she

1. Rodney Dangerfield's Associated Press obituary; Rodney Dangerfield's official Web site bio, www.rodney.com.

2. www.Answers.com: biography listing; www.kfc.com: company history page.

3. www.littlehouseontheprairie.com; www.eduplace.com.

was nearly eighty that her paintings became the toast of the art world.[4]

5 Chef, author, and television personality Julia Child had a career in advertising until her husband's job resulted in a transfer to Paris. At age thirty-nine, she enrolled in a French cooking school; she published her masterpiece, *Mastering the Art of French Cooking,* at age forty-nine. At age fifty-four, Child received an Emmy Award for her television show, *The French Chef,* and continued filming highly rated television shows and specials until she was eighty-seven.[5]

6 Irma B. Elder was born in Mexico and immigrated to the U.S. with her parents as a girl. She was a Michigan housewife and mother when her husband, James, died suddenly in 1983. At age fifty-two, Elder took over her husband's car dealership and built it into Elder Automotive Group, one of the largest and most successful dealerships in the world, as well as one of the top ten largest Hispanic-owned companies in the country.[6]

7 After a successful career in banking, Evelyn Gregory became a flight attendant at the age of seventy-one. Initially rejected by several airlines, she finally fulfilled her childhood dream when she was hired by Mesa Airlines in 1999, where she worked for six years.[7]

---

4. www.Answers.com: biography listing; www.gseart.com: Galerie St. Etienne Web site (New York City gallery that represents Moses's estate).

5. www.Starchefs.com: biography listing; www.Biography.com: listing.

6. www.Detnews.com: *Detroit News,* 2003 Michiganian of the Year profile; www.Nabbw.com: National Association of Baby Boomer Women, column.

7. "Catching up with Evelyn Gregory: In golden years, flying friendly skies," *The Charlotte Observer,* February 2006; www.findarticles.com; www.airlinecareer.com.

4

LEARNING TO LIVE IN THE PRESENT

One of the most tragic things I know about human nature is that all of us tend to put off living. We are all dreaming of some magical rose garden over the horizon—instead of enjoying the roses that are blooming outside our windows today.

Dale Carnegie,
Lecturer and Writer on Self-Improvement

A friend has a heart attack unexpectedly or a relative dies. The guy you knew from work dropped dead on a racquetball court. The son of a neighbor was in a car crash on the freeway. We face mortality every day. It stops us in our tracks for a moment, long enough maybe to think: "Wow. That could have been me!" and make a pledge to ourselves to relax and appreciate life more. Then, five minutes later, we slip right back into the same old routine of not appreciating anything much at all.

I lost my son a few years ago to a senseless, violent death. We'd been estranged for many years but had recently reunited. He was living with me, in my apartment, at the time he was murdered. His death came at the hand of a friend, a guy he'd known most of his life. The reason? A stupid, meaningless fight followed by a spontaneous outburst of fury. Marshawn's death claimed three lives that night: his own, snuffed out forever; his assailant's (imprisoned for fifty years); and another kid's (sentenced to thirty years hard time for his involvement). Neither man has much, if any, hope of parole.

> *We didn't lose the game; we just ran out of time.*
> **Vince Lombardi,**
> **Legendary Football Coach**

I tell you this personal story to underscore the point that, whether white-collar, blue-collar, or no-collar, *tomorrow is not promised to any of us.* Though we may understand this on an "intellectual" level—I mean, we're all gonna die, aren't we?—most of us continue to act as though tomorrow is money in the bank.

It's tough to comprehend that we're only on Earth for the blink of an eye—after all, to us, that's a lifetime—so we squander precious days, months, and years living existences mapped out by inertia, routine, and compromise. We live as though we've got *forever* ahead of us.

Savvy7

LIVE IN THE NOW!

Okay, so you're ready to embrace each and every minute of each and every day. How is it done? Try these tips:

1 **Leave the past behind.** There's nothing you can do to change the past; in fact, the best you can do is provide an apology or reparation if you are in the wrong. Living in the now is about today, not yesterday.

2 **Don't worry or fret about the future.** Remember, tomorrow is not guaranteed. While it's smart to plan for the future, you still need to live for today.

3 **When speaking to others, don't think of what your next witty remark will be.** Instead, actually LISTEN to what the other person is saying. You might be surprised at the opportunities you've been missing.

4 **Do something spontaneous and fun.** Start a water fight with your kids in the backyard, surprise your wife with concert tickets for tonight's show, or try a new recipe for dinner. Spontaneity is *all* about the here and now—try it on for size!

5 **Do something "seasonal."** Eat ripe produce in season, build a snowman, rake leaves into a pile and jump into it. Acknowledging each season will prevent those "where did the year go?" feelings in November and December.

6 **Clear some clutter out of your house!** Packrats aren't just clinging to objects; they're clinging to the past.

7 **Forgive someone who once wronged you.** Harboring anger at someone who's moved on doesn't hurt them— it only hurts you.

*In basketball—as in life—true joy comes from being
fully present in each and every moment.*

**Phil Jackson,
NBA Coach, Nine-Time Champion**

How many times have you heard stories of guys who do everything that's expected of them? They work long and hard. In fact, they spend far more time in the office, on business trips, or commuting to and from the suburbs, than they do with their families. After all, they say: "You've gotta do what you gotta do."

These are the folks who focus their entire lives on their jobs. These loyal corporate citizens move their families and put their kids in schools close to the office or the train station (in case of weekend calls and late nights), and then bank on a secure job taking them into a comfortable retirement.

Problem is you can't bank *tomorrow* and retirement could arrive early, both unexpected and unwelcome.

The Japanese have a name for guys who devote their lives to the company. They're called *salarimen*. Sometimes these hard-working corporate foot soldiers put in forty-plus hours overtime a week (mostly unpaid); they sacrifice themselves for the company. Would you believe they have a name for "death through overwork" in Japan? It is called *karoshi*.

*Do not dwell in the past, do not dream of the future,
concentrate the mind on the present moment.*

**Buddha,
Philosopher and Religious Leader**

Over the years, I've seen many a guy go to an early grave because of some bullshit on the streets, but these days there seems to be more stories of guys running out of steam—and running out of time—in the white-collar world, too.

A while back, an acquaintance of mine who was a senior executive at a major Fortune 500 company died suddenly of a heart attack. He was in his mid-fifties, fit, active, and professionally successful.

Ironically, he'd been promoted that very same day to some senior executive position—finally achieving a lifetime goal that had meant a great deal to him.

For years, he'd worked, worried, and traveled around the clock, stressing his mind and straining his body. He lived in a heightened state, adrenaline gushing like a geyser, as he met one high-pressure deadline after another: important speeches, hard-nosed negotiations, extravagant and complex corporate events, and high profile, high-stakes board meetings. And if that wasn't enough, he hurtled his body between cities, countries, and continents, sitting for hours on end in dim, stuffy airplane cabins, and dim, stuffy meeting rooms, inhaling stale air, carbs, and caffeine!

I wouldn't presume to speculate whether or not he was satisfied with the life he'd carved out for himself, but I do know he exited it far too soon.

He chose to live a stressful, unhealthy life, but for others, choice itself is a luxury. The tough streets of America's 'hoods and barrios are one place where folks get caught up in *catching up*. It's challenging enough just to get through today, they say. With luck, everything will work itself out tomorrow. Religious faith often takes the place of a 401K plan for America's poor, because it's the only "tomorrow" security they can look forward to.

Worse still, some of the kids I grew up with are dead or incarcerated because they couldn't see beyond the *moment*. Caught up in the street survival game without the imagination, education, or resources to forge a path to tomorrow, these kids gave their lives in exchange for a single *moment of satisfaction*.

There are no shortcuts. Success is the journey, not just the destination. To achieve it, we've gotta stop chasing the feel-good-right-now highs that only serve to deflect us from the real end game. We all know, deep down, there are no magic pills that make us rich, satisfied, and fulfilled overnight. If something seems too good to be true, it's because it is.

Whether by choice or necessity, most of us fail to enjoy the present, choosing instead the *mañana trap*; settling for less today and deferring everything good until tomorrow.

We cannot truly face life until we face the fact that it will be taken away from us.

Billy Graham,
Religious Leader and Educator

So somewhere between the stress of today and the vague promise of tomorrow, we have to relearn to live fully in the *present*, the way we did when we were kids. Remember when you were a kid and you tried your hardest at almost everything, every time? Now, that's living! *Time* is priceless and *tomorrow* isn't bankable: Every day is precious; every moment a fresh new dollar that, when it's spent, is spent.

I live with a sharp sense of my own mortality, which in many ways makes life more vivid and immediate.

Anita Roddick,
Founder of The Body Shop

I love life. I'm thankful for every single day that my feet hit the ground in the morning, rain or shine. Every day is my birthday, and I actually anticipate the challenges each fresh day throws my way, because challenge, even adversity, only serves to motivate and drive me to greater heights. What doesn't kill me only makes me stronger!

Being Streetwise requires that you develop an appetite for living. Once you understand that every minute counts, you'll begin to respond to each day with new urgency. When you feel the *need* to squeeze every last drop of the "good stuff" from life—that's when you'll be ready to add some serious hustle to your game!

For a long time, it had seemed to me that life was about to begin—real life. But there was always some obstacle in the way, something to be gotten through first, some unfinished business, time still to be served, a debt to be paid. Then life would begin. At last it dawned on me that these obstacles were my life.

Father Alfred D'Souza

NO ARTIFICIAL ADDITIVES REQUIRED

Doing the best at this moment puts you in the best place for the next moment.

Oprah Winfrey,
Media Mogul

REAL TALK

My friend Jessica thinks she's rewarding herself by enjoying a drink or two at the end of each workday. Now true, lots of folks have a drink to wind down and relax. Problem is, these days, two cocktails have become three or four (or Jessica loses count) . . . and the drinks are getting stiffer, too. She loves alcohol's nice warm buzz, the way it melts away her troubles, and how it gives her something to really look forward to.

But she sure as heck doesn't look forward to the mornings after. Jessica feels half dead when the alarm goes off—she even slept right through it recently. And best believe, that girl looks as wrecked as she feels. She used to practically bounce her fit body to the gym every morning before work. Now she can barely drag herself, and those extra pounds, to the office on time.

Jessica's no fool—she knows she's selling herself short, but she just can't seem to find the willpower to get back on track.

Many of us can relate to Jessica's story, and for my part, it's no secret that for years I poured all kinds of poisonous crap into my body. It's not something I'm proud of, but it is part of the fabric that's Burrel.

You know those horror stories about teens and pre-teens, who begin using drugs on the regular at a startling age? Well, folks, I was one of those kids—at least, until I gave it all up at age sixteen.

Why did I treat myself so badly for years? For the same reason most folks turn to substance abuse, whether it's weed, pills, alcohol, or even food: to dumb down (and forget) or sharpen up.

For me, it was all about trying to enhance my life in some way. I wanted to be sharper and faster than everyone around me, and I thought I needed drugs to help me do that. I took drugs to rev up my mind and my body, followed by more drugs to quiet and calm, followed by more drugs to get rid of the drowsy side effects, followed by more drugs to combat the jitters and paranoia. Round and round it went. A never-ending, potentially deadly cycle.

And, of course, I couldn't have been more wrong:

- Rather than make me stronger, this chemical cycle made me weaker.

- Rather than clear my mind, it clouded it.

- Rather than quicken my reflexes, it slowed me down.

- Rather than improve my life, it nearly ended it.

> *Why is there so much controversy about drug testing?*
> *I know plenty of guys who would be willing to test any*
> *drug they could come up with.*
> **George Carlin,**
> **Comedian**

No, that part of my life was not my finest hour—but here's something I AM proud of: *by channeling all my willpower, I was able to kick a habit that was dulling my senses, killing my brain cells, and leaving my body as damaged and dry as scorched earth.*

Today I revel in the sharpness and clarity of my mind. I have a heightened sense of pleasure and appreciation for life. I love the strength and power of my body, and I enjoy incredibly full, rich relationships.

Most of all, I love living fully in the present with all its sharp edges, bright colors, and glitter, rather than in some movie shot underwater with fuzzy edges and a muffled soundtrack. Do I enjoy a glass of wine or champagne every now and again? You bet, though not often. Makes me feel too flaky the next day, and I won't allow anything to get in the way of my exercise routine, which to me is the ultimate paycheck for my mind, body, and spirit.

We'll talk quite a bit more about this later, but here's some advice from a guy who knows: dump those bad habits. You don't need them. There are better approaches (all natural) that are guaranteed to make you feel strong, relaxed, energized, and ready to tackle just about anything!

No artificial additives required, thank you!

I continued to get high, and low, and high again, whenever I could. Ironically, by transporting me into my own private world, my diet of uppers and downers enabled me to carve out slices of space for meditation and introspection. Such moments were often accompanied by unwelcome clarity.

I used this headroom for some straight talking. I told myself that soon I was going to give all this up; that I'd buy one respectable business or another, and stop hanging out on street corners, taking stupid risks and doing wrong.

Uncompromisingly tough, I berated myself endlessly for the damage I was causing to myself and others and for still being in the game, when I knew I should long since have left it behind.

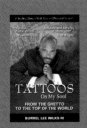

So, somewhat paradoxically, taking drugs created oases of calm in the midst of my crazy, frenetic, jittery, paranoid world, and I used those *quiet* times to talk myself *out* of taking drugs. I felt like I was watching my own struggle on TV, a young foolish guy scrabbling for sense.—From *Tattoos on My Soul*

5

SOMETIMES THE RULES WILL SET YOU FREE

I was never much for rules, anyway; otherwise, I probably wouldn't have invented anything or gone so far in music.

Les Paul,
Electric Guitar Innovator

When I was a kid, I hated rules of any kind. Unfortunately, for me, we had quite a few of them in my house. My dad was real *ol' skool,* a hard core OG [Old Gangster: a term of respect for guys who came from an older generation of "real players"]. He ran a pretty tight ship and asserted his authority at home in the same uncompromising way he did on the streets. Man, oh man, did we have rules.

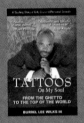

Boss of the streets, my old man was a despot at home. An unbending disciplinarian who made sure we all danced to his tune. He was ol' skool and some. The Highway Code had fewer rules than we did at home. We couldn't play ball on the street, walk on the grass, have friends sit on the porch, eat too much cereal, or play tag. In fact, most the activities in which a boisterous boy loves to get tangled up were forbidden under my dad's roof.

The man with the X-ray eyes, perpetually scanning his fiefdom, never missed a thing at home or on the streets. He reserved the toughest scrutiny of all for those closest to him. Burrel Senior practiced some of the toughest tough-love imaginable.

Dad wrote all the rules and was uncompromising in their enforcement, by hand, boot, or belt! I was thrashed—probably hundreds of times. An irrepressibly naughty boy with the stubbornness of a bull and the thick head to match, I was constantly in trouble, my infractions too many to list.

> I'd dip into Dad's money, smoke his weed, track mud onto the carpet, break a cup, or empty the cereal box. I'd be caught fighting, playing hooky, walking on the grass, stealing my brother's birthday money—you name it, I was probably guilty of it. As a consequence of my relentless mischievousness, I faced the full force of Dad's fury more frequently than anyone else.—From *Tattoos on My Soul*

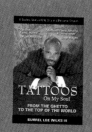

Being the independent person that I was, I naturally rebelled as I grew older and tried to challenge my father's highly regimented world. I mean, with my old man and me living under the same roof—two bull-headed, iron-willed individuals—things were bound to come to a head, and before long they did. On my sixteenth birthday, I moved out of the family home to do my own thing and answer to no one but myself.

It came as bit of a surprise then, even to me, when, having finally escaped out from under my dad's thumb, I started disciplining myself. Instead of my dad kickin' my ass, I began kickin' it myself! I discovered early on that having a strong belief system to guide me—rules of engagement for life, if you will—was, in fact, a *help*, not a *hindrance*, *liberating*, not *inhibiting*. So even as I tore up one rule book, I began writing a whole new one.

Rule your mind or it will rule you.

Horace,
Philosopher

Over the years, as I logged experience and learned some tough life lessons through trial and error, instinct, and emulation, I unconsciously formulated a set of strategies that began to shape how I lived. These *Streetwise Strategies* became the guidelines for my personal behavior, my relationships, my day-to-day activities, and my longer-term "career" decisions. Ultimately, they provided the personal compass that made it possible for me to make my transformation from gang chief to life coach, author, and legitimate businessman.

THE BONUSES OF LIVING WITH RULES

*It's not hard to make decisions
when you know what your values are.*

**Roy Disney,
Filmmaker and Theme Park Entrepreneur**

Ah, the blessed relief of not having to battle with yourself every day. I discovered that my new rule book came with some valuable and unexpected bonuses. You see, when you set parameters for yourself and choose which lines you refuse to cross, it becomes *easier* to stay on a chosen path.

Think about it. How much time do you spend wrestling emotionally with yourself every day? Here are some examples of simple everyday, energy-sapping dilemmas:

- "I know I should go to the gym. But, I'm so stressed out I really don't feel up to it. I know it would make me feel better, and I did promise myself that I'd get back on my workout schedule this week. Still, I do deserve a break—I mean it's been a tough week and I should take it easy on myself. But, on the other hand . . ."

- "I know I should tell him what I think of him. I just don't want to cause problems. I mean, if I upset him, he could make my life hell. I know it's not a bed of roses now, but he could make it a lot worse. Life's too hard to make waves, isn't it? On the other hand . . ."

Round and round it goes.

We all have these circular arguments with ourselves, and frankly, they're energy sapping and pointless. Instead of endlessly procrastinating and second-guessing yourself, how much easier would it be if you already had the answer figured out?

As I've said before, my sixteenth year was a big one. It was the year I finally understood what it would take to move my life forward. And

41

with this clarity came decisiveness. I no longer expended my time or effort trying to figure out what to do, because that was now obvious. Instead, I could channel all that energy into actually doing it! By focusing my considerable resources on kicking my deadly narcotic habit and turning my life 180 degrees, I was able to leave home, stay off the streets, and leverage myself out of gang life and into a new world. At the time, my new take-charge, sober world was as alien to this streetwise *shorty* as Earth must have seemed to ET!

In short, I transformed *helplessness* into *hopefulness*.

By the age of sixteen, I'd come a long way in formulating my personal belief system—my rules of engagement. Gone was the need to debate endlessly with myself about anything. The answers were now crystal clear. It was the kind of clarity that sliced through confusion like a knife through butter and shone light into the darkest corners of my mind, scaring out that enemy called Doubt wherever he lurked.

With the ejection of doubt comes an additional (and colossal) benefit: when you remove doubt, you eliminate fear. And without fear to hold you back, you'll be completely re-energized. Life seems both simpler and more wonderful. Boundaries disappear, obstacles shrink, and it's as though you're running down the mountainside, free and clear, instead of gasping and struggling up its icy, dicey north face!

"DEBATE OVER!"

*Be willing to make decisions. That's the most
important quality in a good leader. Don't fall victim
to what I call the "ready-aim-aim-aim-aim syndrome."
You must be willing to fire.*

**George S. Patton,
Military Leader**

"**D**ebate over." Two of the most powerful words you'll ever hear—especially when they echo convincingly inside your own head.

Do you remember the arguments you used to have with your parents when you were a kid? At bedtime, mealtime, or school time? Perhaps they're the same kind of "discussions" you have with your own kids today?

Your mother would say it was time for bed, or that, no, you couldn't have any more spending money, miss school, or stay out late. You'd launch a counterattack dredging up every reason under the sun as to why you should be allowed to do what you want, or why you shouldn't have to do what your mother wants. Begging, whining, and throwing the occasional tantrum, you and your mom would get into it like a verbal tag-team match. Then, just as you thought you were making headway—winning, even—your mom or dad would get that steely look in their eye and declare: "That's it. Enough already. Debate over!"

And right away, you knew that it was.

Now these two little words, "Debate over," are going to be put to work for you. You see, the toughest part of success is *deciding* to be successful, and making and sticking to the smaller decisions that become the building blocks for larger-scale success. So while you may allow yourself the luxury of procrastination at first, at some point you have to draw a line in the sand, declare "Debate over"—and get moving!

*The critical ingredient is getting off your butt
and doing something. It's as simple as that.
A lot of people have ideas, but there are few
who decide to do something about them now.
Not tomorrow. Not next week. But today.
The true entrepreneur is a doer, not a dreamer.*

**Nolan Bushnell,
Video Game Entrepreneur**

IF NO ONE ELSE WILL, KICK YOUR OWN ASS!

If you take too long in deciding what to do
with your life, you'll find you've done it.

George Bernard Shaw,
Nobel Prize-Winning Author and Playwright

Still struggling with willpower issues?

Ever since I was a teenager, I've kicked my own ass when I needed to. Strange, but true. It happened first when I gave up the habit of substance abuse. I arrived at a point one day, when I knew, without a doubt, that I was going to die very soon unless something changed fast. I remember the moment well. I was lying in bed, half asleep, suffering from some kind of chemical hangover, drifting in and out of consciousness when suddenly, with stark, shocking clarity, I saw my own funeral.

I believe passionately in mind power, and I understand that our brains work on both a conscious and unconscious level. We'll be talking more about that later, but as I was stumbling through the painful process of self-discovery, it appeared my brain had been working on some creative processing of its own. While I had been mumbling, snorting, and sleeping, my mind had been taking a long hard look at the threads of my life and drawing its own conclusions. Now it was ready to share the results with me, and the picture was not a pretty one. I knew from that moment onward, if I didn't turn my life around I would die. Simple as that.

I made the decision right then and there, in my bed, to reprogram the old Burrel and get a grip on *living*, not *dying*. Once that goal was firmly in my sights, I was locked and loaded. The moment I told myself, "Debate over," it truly was over. I was like a heat-seeking missile, a man on a *mission*. I kicked my habit, and whenever I was tempted to pick it up again, I kicked myself in the ass. Literally.

Now I'm certainly not suggesting you physically beat yourself up. There are many ways to give yourself a virtual ass-kickin'. Try depriving yourself of your favorite food, commit to a 10k run for a charity, give yourself some additional chores, or set up a regular allotment into a savings account (that can't be touched for ten years). Put your money where your mouth is and, above all, don't let yourself off the hook.

On one hand, I'm a great believer that we should be kind to ourselves—because goodness knows, life sometimes isn't. But when being good *to yourself*, means being bad *for yourself*, then it's time to shift gears. Sure, that trip through the drive-thru might taste good today, but it will leave a rotten taste in your mouth when your pants don't fit tomorrow. And who knows—you may even find that the punishment is really the prize.

SO, WHAT ARE YOUR RULES OF ENGAGEMENT?

Unless you try to do something beyond what you have already mastered, you will never grow.

Ronald E. Osborn,
Theologian

Lots of folks turn to faith or family when they need emotional, spiritual, or moral direction. Hats off to them, for having a structured belief system. Some of us may be spiritually aware and hold equally strong values, but our belief system looks kinda like a beater car you'd see in the 'hood or the country. You know the type: painted blue, except for the red hood, brown door, and primer gray patch in the back. And the back bumper's missing. And there's a pair of pliers where the door handle should be. And the radio doesn't work.

Otherwise, it's in great shape, right? Runs, don't it?

See, that car is like a personal belief system made up of bits and pieces of wisdom, philosophy, and religious doctrine picked up along the path of life, with no concern for the finished product. We should all design our own code of beliefs, but it's crucial that all the pieces add up to something that can *really* propel us along the road to success.

It's true, too, that some of the values we learned from our parents—our *legacy values*—might not be so relevant these days, or don't apply to the adult lives we've created for ourselves. Many Americans have parents or grandparents who emigrated from another country, and find values from "the old country" at odds with the way things are done today in the U.S. One thing's for sure, in our generation's media-obsessed, globally accessible, messy, conflicting world, nothing appears to be straightforward or simple anymore (although, in reality, most things are).

In my opinion, it takes a lot of hard living and hard lessons to arrive at a clear set of life rules. And it takes even more practice before they develop into success strategies. So no, it's not enough to believe *only* what our parents, teachers, and spiritual leaders tell us; we must supplement that with our own "custom" beliefs.

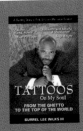

Like most people, my faith is made up of a mosaic of beliefs, not a single formula. I'm deeply spiritual but not religious. I meditate, lost within myself or in the clouds and stars, for hours on end. My faith sustains me. I feel privileged and blessed to be alive and healthy. There is a reason I'm still here. I intend to make the most of the energy, insight, and knowledge I have been blessed with to positively influence the lives of others. I sense patterns in the universe, a fatalistic faith that has helped me cope with the vicissitudes of life.—From *Tattoos on My Soul*

Some of us never get so far as to define our own rules of engagement. Perhaps we think we're too busy, cynical, or tired. Or even worse, perhaps we simply can't be bothered to make the effort. Maybe we even enjoy ricocheting our way through life, like a ball-bearing tearing up a pinball machine. It's certainly one way to do it, but if that's the path you've chosen, you'd better be prepared for more than a few black eyes and broken noses!

In the end, the key to unlocking success for life is less about knowing the theory of what you *should* be doing, and more about focusing your resources on *actually doing* it. A belief system allows you to do just that by helping you free up emotional energy so that all this power can be rechanneled into getting results.

I met DeAndre, a.k.a. Black, at the gym. He's a hard guy to miss: a fit, good-looking brother who many people say looks a little like Michael Jordan. Black was already a somewhat successful guy when I met him. Although he had grown up poor, he had managed to already acquire a piece of real estate as an investment, and he wasn't even yet thirty years old.

REAL TALK

But still, Black wasn't the giant he was meant to be. For one, he was letting some poisonous people hold him back. His girlfriend was sucking him dry, demanding he spend more money on her than he could really afford. He was also having problems leaving his not-so-successful friends behind in the 'hood. They were making him feel guilty for movin' up, the way haters do, and he was having a hard time choosing his own success over the affections of his so-called friends.

But Black's biggest problem was that he was living his life according to his parents' values, not his own. Now, Black may have grown up poor, but his family wasn't destitute. His mother made a nice home, and there was always plenty of food on the table. Both of his parents were employed, but they were stuck in dead-end jobs. They had worker mentalities, and they passed those on to their son.

Problem was, Black wasn't like his parents. He was a hustler at heart. Even as a kid, he was one of those *shorties* you see standing outside the supermarket, selling candy bars to earn money. He had an entrepreneurial spirit, but he lacked the proper rule structure to make his dreams a reality. His legacy values were making him settle for less when

REAL TALK

it came to business dealings, sticking with low-risk investments with low payouts, and taking the first price he was offered. In the expensive Los Angeles real estate market, that could mean leaving hundreds of thousands of dollars on the table.

Once he cleared away the negative people in his life, I taught him that a businessman or woman can be warm and respectful, yet still ask for and get what they need. He learned to carry himself more confidently and assertively in negotiations, but still play fair and be positive. And I taught him to hold off until he could get the best deal, and walk away if the deal wasn't good for him.

Now Black is in the business of rehabilitating old apartment buildings, which is not only profitable but rewarding. And his mother is so proud of him, too!

SUCCESS

Part2

Making Your Mind Your Greatest Ally

You'll only fly as high as your mind allows—that is, if you allow your mind to fly! Build your mental strength. Get that mental muscle in the best shape it can be!

6

GETTING MENTALLY FIT FOR SUCCESS

*Two men look out
the same prison bars;
one sees mud and the other stars.*

Frederick Langbridge,
Poet

Film buffs among us may have seen the story of the "Great Escape" dramatized in the 1963 movie by the same name. It's a great movie starring one of the ultimate individualists of all time and a real Giant: Steve McQueen. In this infamous true story, seventy-six prisoners of war, all dedicated "escapees," broke out of a German-controlled concentration camp during the deep winter of 1944.

Through courage, ingenuity, and back-breaking, heart-breaking effort, these seventy-six men succeeded in tunneling their way out of prison that freezing March and escaping into the German countryside, before scattering in all directions. All but three were recaptured and nearly all were executed: a terrible end to a truly heroic story that was noted in history as one of the most magnificent gestures of defiance of World War II.

Would you have made a break for it against those odds? The pragmatist in me says "no," while the defiant, relentless optimist says "yes." We'd all like to think of ourselves as brave escapees. After all, this is a country where "free" folks look down with pity—contempt even—on the millions incarcerated for real, locked up behind bars with no fresh air to breath, no sun or stars above, and no liberty left to them.

Yup, we pride ourselves on being a nation of freedom-loving individualists, a people who rate freedom as highly as anything and who will defend it to the death. Strange then, that so many of us appear to be intent on replicating those very same "penitentiary conditions" in our own lives every day!

What on Earth do I mean?

Well, think about it. We exist within our own prison cells every day. The difference is that our walls are built with worry and sealed with stress. We're fenced in, not by concrete or barbed wire but by low self-worth, expensive lifestyles, debt, peer pressure, and poor relationships. Worse still, once we're safely walled inside whatever little mental and lifestyle cell we've constructed, we tell ourselves this is our only option and toss away the key. Face it: we don't just put ourselves in jail; we appoint ourselves prison warden, too!

And over time, we become institutionalized. It takes more and more effort to even peer over the top of the walls, so we don't bother trying anymore. Too busy and distracted to see beyond today's "to-do list," we squeeze our lives into the small space we've allotted and settle for it—before we even realize that's what we've done.

The man who has no imagination has no wings.
Muhammad Ali,
Boxing Heavyweight Champion of the World

I can't tell you how many guys from my old neighborhood fall into the trap of self-imprisonment. Life in the inner city is harsh on a good day, but like us all, these guys also set out through life with big dreams and boastful ambitions. Problem is, after years of hitting brick wall after brick wall, being knocked back and down one time too many, understandably they run out of steam, settling instead for simply getting through each day the best they can.

But in the end, the environment in which you operate makes little difference because we're each as susceptible as the next man to *the trap of compromise.* It has little to do with your habitat: whether you spend your days at home, on the factory floor, or in an office cubicle, it's not your environment that constrains you, but your mind. You see, it's easier to slip into a comfortable mental rut and stay there, rather than keep fighting to climb out. Because getting out of a rut—your mental jail cell—requires changing thought patterns, adjusting behaviors, and, ultimately, creating new habits. Like it or not, that takes hard work. Understandably, it's tough to find the necessary perspective, energy, and momentum required to get started.

Few of us are prepared to take risks with our well-planned, well-ordered lives anyway, so rather than disrupt things by making a mental "break for it," we just keep doin' what we're doin'.

We settle for living in a box.
And as we settle, our dreams, ambitions, and optimism
get squeezed in and pressed down
in that box with us.

Burrel

YOUR MIND: WORST ENEMY OR BEST FRIEND?

*Your opponent, in the end, is never really the player
on the other side of the net, or the swimmer in the
next lane, or the team on the other side of the field, or
even the bar you must high-jump. Your opponent is
yourself, your negative internal voices, and your level
of determination.*

**Grace Lichtenstein,
Author and Journalist**

It helps to know your enemy. And the good news is you're already on intimate terms with him or her, because your most dangerous enemy is, of course, YOU. Yup, inevitably the worst culprit when it comes to holding us back is ourselves. Now the good news is, you also know your greatest ally pretty well, too. You guessed it—that would be YOU again!

Your own worst enemy or very best friend? Which one would YOU rather be? The choice is entirely yours.

Now I want you to stand in front of the mirror and take a good hard look at yourself. What kind of self-image do you carry inside your head? Think of it this way: if you were to have a conversation with your other self, your alter ego, what would you say to him or her about his or her life? And if the situation was reversed and your alter ego were giving you advice, what would you expect to hear him or her say?

*The mind is the limit. As long as the mind can
envision the fact that you can do something, you can
do it, as long as you really believe 100 percent.*

**Arnold Schwarzenegger,
Actor, Body-building Legend, Governor of California**

Would this *reflected* you be patting the *real* you on the back and telling you what a great job you're doing? Or would he or she want to kick your ass over all the missed opportunities that you've passed up so far? I hope your alter ego would be kind to you, but I suspect you may have an ass-kickin' in store!

What is it about us? Why are we always our own worst critics? Why do we usually see ourselves in such a negative light compared to everyone else (those others who always seem to be richer, smarter, thinner, and happier than we are)? Why does that voice inside our head sabotage us at every turn, telling us we can't change and won't succeed? Why do we find it so hard to love and accept ourselves?

Fear, low self-esteem, conditioning, whatever our personal reasons, the more negative the movie in our heads, the more negative our lives are going to be.

I work with a number of NBA players. Think any of them make a three-pointer by telling themselves: "It won't go in. I just know it won't go in!" Not a chance. All that player sees in his mind is perfection: a vision of him jumping up, getting mad air, releasing a picture-perfect shot, the ball swooshing through the net, and the crowd going wild.

If you've got negative pictures swirling around inside your head, it's time to change the channel and turn yourself from enemy to ally!

Burrel

SEVEN MAJOR MENTAL ROADBLOCKS

The only one who can tell you "you can't" is you. And you don't have to listen. You're the one who put up these mental roadblocks. So you can drive right through them.

- **Roadblock #1: "I don't need to change."** A lot of folks don't feel they need to change. They either don't realize they are out of step or they believe everyone else is! These are guys who believe they get it, and everyone else is either wrong or stupid. I was in a meeting recently with about twenty others listening to a presentation. No one could understand where the heck the presenter was coming from, but he was the one getting mad because none of us understood him. It's true that sometimes when you're far ahead of the pack, you'll be misunderstood, and that can be frustrating, but make sure you *are* ahead—not behind! If you're consistently out of step with everyone else, it may be time to change the dance!

- **Roadblock #2: "Change is scary."** People usually get caught in a groove for a reason: *they like it there.* Problem is there's not a lot of difference between a groove and a rut, and though these people may complain about feeling "stuck," at least it's a familiar and comfortable kind of "stuck"; a nice, warm dead-end. Trouble is, if you stay put and never try to see what's on the other side of that wall, you might miss something good, something beautiful—something that makes your life special.

- **Roadblock #3: "Change is hard work."** I can sure relate to this one. After all, I'm a man who's transformed himself many times already, from gang chief to entrepreneur and business-man to life coach, author, motivator, and advocate. Heck, yes, it's hard work! Changing embedded behaviors and negative self-perception, prizing open a clam-like mind, heaving your-self out of your nice warm comfort zone, that all takes some serious mental heavy lifting. But what's the alternative? Sticking your head in the sand and hoping it'll all sort itself out? Trust me, it won't.

- **Roadblock #4: "The people around me keep dragging me back."** In the world from which I come—the inner city streets—this kind of *player hating* is one of the greatest killers of personal progress, and unfortunately, it's all too common. I've seen it played out hundreds of times in all walks of life. Fact is, when folks see you movin' on, they feel like they're being left behind. They get scared—or jealous—and may try and drag you backward so you can keep them company. Even the most tightly knit, loving families can prove to be *success blockers*. The thing is, when we change, it compels the people around us to change, too. And because they won't be in the same state of mental readiness as you, their natural response will be to push back. We'll talk more about how to identify *poisonous people* in chapter 8.

> *No man is ever whipped, until he quits—*
> *in his own mind.*
>
> **Napoleon Hill,**
> **Author**

- **Roadblock #5: "I'm too busy or stressed."** Excuses are like noses. We all have 'em. If you're not prepared to make the time for change, then you might as well stop complainin' about life right now. If success isn't important enough for you to prioritize, then you've already settled for second-best. We get *one inning*. You can sit it out or play to win. Your call.

- **Roadblock #6: "I don't know where to start."** Pursuing success and embracing personal change is a daunting task. With all the everyday pressures and conflicting advice, where do you begin? The best place to start is inside. In reality, you probably already have a good idea of what you need to do, but the knowledge is either hidden deep amidst all your day-to-day frustrations or buried under the weight of denial. The good news, however, is that humans are naturally goal-oriented creatures. (We'll spend more time exploring how to get your arms around your goals in chapter 9.)

● **Roadblock #7: " I don't know what success looks like."** It's not unusual to struggle with this. After all, when you're still viewing the world through the same eyes as yesterday and the day before that, it's tough to visualize a fresh perspective. For now, instead of focusing on what needs to *change*, focus on what *outcomes* you want. We'll cover some great mind-movie techniques later to help you unlock the power of your imagination.

The *Biggest Roadblock* of all? Doing nothing at all.

> *That's why many fail—because they don't get started—they don't go. They don't overcome inertia. They don't begin.*
>
> **W. Clement Stone,**
> **Self-help Book Author**

YA GOTTA DO IT

GETTING MENTALLY FIT FOR SUCCESS

What kind of qualities do you look for in a friend? Write down three. Now, flip the script: do you show these qualities toward yourself? YOU must be your own best friend if you want to succeed, so start applying those three qualities to the way you treat yourself and adjust your inner dialogue accordingly.

7

FREE YOUR MIND (THE REST WILL FOLLOW!)

A mind, once stretched
by a new idea, never regains
its original dimensions.

Oliver Wendell Holmes,
U.S. Supreme Court Justice

THROW OUT THE "COULDA-SHOULDA'S"

*A weak mind is like a microscope, which magnifies
trifling things, but cannot receive great ones.*
Lord Chesterfield

Go and dig out some of your old family snapshots. I know you've got
'em tucked in corners all over the place, or stuffed into some "photo
box" at the back of the closet. Or perhaps, if you're more organized
than I am, you might even have them displayed neatly and chrono-
logically in a set of photo albums on the bookshelf.

Take a moment to randomly pull out a few images. Chances are
you have one or two favorites sitting around in photo frames anyway, but I'm betting when you dig out those old photos, the ones
you don't usually see, a couple of them will stop you in your tracks.
There's something deeply poignant about catching a glimpse of your
past—even if you have no urge to revisit that time in your life. The
flood of memories, the fleeting sensation of moments lived, emotions experienced, people touched, and roads traveled can really
sucker punch ya.

Here you are in a school line-up or looking totally eighties as
you get ready for a night out on the town. There's a picture of you
and your mom, or dad, or siblings, or best friends, at a wedding, on
a beach, at a street party, looking awkward, happy, shy, sullen, surprised—makes you smile, doesn't it?

I gravitate toward those snapshots of myself when I was a real
shorty—even before I hit my teens. There's something about these
images that affects me deeply. It's as though I'm some other guy
looking at a picture of a little boy he used to know well, far in his
past; a little boy who somehow touches an emotional chord deep
inside the man standing here today.

Yup, those sure were the days.

I had my own pad in the basement of our house, not as a teenager
but as a nine-year-old shorty. My apartment became the epicenter for

the neighborhood crew, and we'd get into all kinds of things—good, not so good, and positively bad! But mostly, we simply partied. Night after night, we'd step dance and sing to Barry White, James Brown, and some cool, cool reggae. The year was 1976. It's a long story told more fully in my memoirs, but I have to say, at nine years old, with little maturity or self-awareness to hamper me, I was having a ball!

Seems as though we had longer, hotter summers in those days. In reality, probably not so, but that's what time does, isn't it? It softens the edges, warms the colors, and papers over the cracks of memories. What strikes me most when I look at photographs of these cocky, young men I once hung with—boys, really, with the world at their feet and immortality in their eyes—is that even as someone's finger pressed down, the shutter blinked, and an image was captured, life had already moved on. Before any one of those smiling kids even heard the camera click, that moment was already history. And before the photograph was developed, new courses would be set, paths taken, life-changing decisions made. The boys in that shot would never be the same again as they were in that split-second captured on glossy paper; some of those smiling faces would never even make it to become grown men.

There are very few of us who don't have a sense of something lost when we look back at the past. Separation from family or friends perhaps; regret for years and youth that can never be recaptured; lost opportunities and bad choices; things we didn't do, and things we did; chances that slipped through our fingers . . .

To be wronged is nothing
unless you continue to remember it.

Confucius,
Philosopher

It's okay to be mildly regretful as long as you just let those feelings play out in the background of your mind, like an old home video, just a sentimental indulgence. Problem is, most of us drag the baggage of yesteryear, as well as the worries of tomorrow, along with us wherever we go. Weighed down by such a heavy load, too often we miss what's offered today. We spend our time either peering ahead with narrowed, skeptical eyes or looking back over our shoulders. We live in the past or the future but seldom in the *moment*.

My wife tells me that sometimes, when she has an important meeting, she'll ask everyone participating to take a moment to share what's on their minds as they enter the room. The everyday things, like worries about a daughter taking a test, or missing a son's football game, or an impending visit from the in-laws. Seems trivial, but when people are allowed to get these "hidden" loads off their chests—baggage they may not even have realized they'd brought into the room with them—they can focus on today's business with new energy and concentration. It makes for more productive meetings.

It's the same with life. Take some time. Clear some head space. Allow yourself a moment to reflect on all the *coulda-shoulda's*. Bask in the glow of nostalgia or wallow in some self-pity. Play the old tunes and indulge your regrets for a moment, a day, or even a week. Then draw a line in the sand, dump the baggage, and get on with the journey. Because what's really important? *Making the most of every moment you have left,* because if you don't, by tomorrow, today will be just another disappointment.

LOSE THE TUNNEL VISION

*A narrow mind and a fat head invariably come
on the same person.*

**Zig Ziglar,
Author and Motivational Speaker**

The guys in that story of the Great Escape I mentioned earlier escaped their prison by way of a tunnel. Unfortunately, for many of us, we spend most of our lives digging in the opposite direction and tunneling our way *into* prison. And while we're in that tunnel, it's the only thing we're thinking about. Whatever our reasons—family, upbringing, education, conforming to social and peer pressure, or simple intellectual laziness—the majority of us tend to look at the world through a pretty narrow lens.

Makes it tough on ourselves.

When you only see a narrow, single-lane road ahead, it leaves little room for maneuvering. When you go into a tunnel and focus only on the light at the other end, it makes you blind to pretty much everything else.

*We think too small.
Like the frog at the bottom of the well. He thinks the sky
is only as big as the top of the well. If he surfaced, he
would have an entirely different view.*

**Mao Tse-Tung,
Military and Political Leader**

Years ago, when traveling overseas, I saw a TV commercial promoting the "journalistic values" of a national daily newspaper published in Britain. The commercial was cool and did a nice job of demonstrating how, when we view a situation through the tunnel vision of narrow thinking, we limit our ability for interpretation and imagination—sometimes dangerously so.

The story went like this: A tough street kid (he's probably the reason the ad caught my attention in the first place) is running fast, down a street, toward an old woman. You just know he's gonna rob her. The tension mounts. He gets closer and closer and, sure enough, violently flings himself at the old lady, knocking her clean off her feet! We, the onlookers, are not at all surprised, of course. As she hits the ground, we know this is exactly what this thug was destined to do. After all, he's a thug, isn't he? So vindicated, we pat ourselves on the back and congratulate ourselves on being so darn perceptive . . .

Now, switch the camera position to the other end of the street and roll back the movie footage a few seconds. Yes, there's the same kid still hurtling, full tilt toward the old lady . . . but wait! From this end of the street, we can now see that the old woman is standing directly in the path of a runaway truck, and this young kid, our accused mugger, is racing to *save* her. His intention is to push her out of harm's way! In fact, he puts his own life on the line in order to save hers. Running head-on into the path of possible death, he gives his all to save a complete stranger (or maybe she was his grandmother . . . remember, this is about assumptions).

My reason for sharing this anecdote is to illustrate the danger of tunnel vision. It vividly demonstrates how tunnel vision hinders us from seeing life in full, glorious, 3-D Technicolor. When you already think you *know* what you're going to see, then that's most likely what you *will* see.

> *We don't see things as they are;*
> *we see them as we are.*
>
> **Anais Nin,**
> **Author**

Tunnel vision is most limiting of all when we turn it in on ourselves. If we wear blinders to survey all that goes on *outside* of us, then it stands to reason we're not going to see too clearly when we look *inside* either. If we don't appreciate the promise on the outside, then how on Earth will we recognize our inner potential?

STOP CRASHING INTO THE LAWN MOWER!

*The mind is like a parachute—
it works only when it is open.*

Unknown

Repetition is not the same thing as persistence. Thinking the same thoughts and taking the same actions over and over isn't going to change a darn thing. Tenacity isn't about beating your head against the same point on the same wall each and every day, in the hope that eventually the wall will crack. No, there are other words for describing that: "plain dumb."

Speaking of plain dumb, a friend of mine had a dog, one of those big hairy, gray-and-white old English sheepdogs. Each morning, Jack would open the front door to let the dog outside, and each morning, without fail, the dog would race through the door, full-speed, and crash head-on into the riding lawn mower parked in front of the house!

My friend thought the dog would learn his lesson after nearly busting its skull open in the first collision; but, no, the next day, and the next, and the one after that, the pattern repeated itself. Door opens, dog rushes out, near concussion. Eventually, Jack had to move the mower.

Now to smart folks like us, it's obvious this isn't persistence; it's stupidity (though I guess the dog eventually got a good result). If it's so obvious then, why do I see otherwise intelligent people doing exactly the same thing every day? Why, when faced with a challenge, do some people throw themselves at it, in a full-frontal assault, again and again, instead of trying to find a route around, over, or even under?

Go on, admit it. How many times have you vowed to: stop getting riled by your boss, stop acting jealous, quit nagging the kids, save more money, start that diet one more time, change your job, spend more time with the family, really use that gym membership this year, work smarter, say "no" more often and drink less—or any one of the above?

And despite those promises to yourself, how many times do you find yourself stressing over the same things every night, hitting the same brick walls, and consistently finding yourself falling back into the same old patterns of behavior that caused you to fail the first time around?

Maybe we're not so different from that dumb dog after all.

Take a quick inventory of your New Year's resolutions. Odds are pretty good they're similar to the ones you made the year before. And the year before that, too. Okay, you argue: I didn't succeed last year because a few things got in the way, but this year it'll be different because I'm more committed than ever.

And so, you make another run at the lawn mower.

TAKE OFF YOUR BRAIN BLINDERS

You have brains in your head.
You have feet in your shoes. You can steer yourself any
direction you choose.

Dr. Seuss,
from *Oh, the Places You'll Go!*

My wife's a traveler. A Brit, she lived for many years in Europe and Asia, before finally settling here in the States. She's traveled to more than forty countries and has never lost her passion for experiencing new and different cultures.

She's got some pretty crazy ideas—in my book anyway—about relaxation and recreation. She says her best vacation ever was a three-week stint in Burma, camping on the beach, in an undeveloped region of the country. She kayaked and trekked—including spending one day tracking a family of elephants through muddy mangrove swamps, at times waist-deep in muck—before heading north, to experience the wonders of the rich culture and extraordinary people.

While I promise you won't (ever!) catch me knee-deep in mangrove mud (it took me long enough to extract myself from my own swamp, thank you), there's no question that travel has helped open my eyes and mind. I've always been curious, of course, and traveled extensively, but mostly in a rather functional kind of way. You know, just doin' what I had to do to get from Point A to Point B.

Whether criss-crossing the country to play golf—which I did almost full time for several years—or heading to Monaco to buy diamonds (I fell in love with that aristocratic playground), I tended to "get in and get out" and seldom spent time hangin' around, simply soakin' up the experience.

My wife taught me a whole new way to look at travel. It's not about airports and lost luggage, bad weather and overbooked hotels, languages you don't understand, and food you don't want to eat. None of that matters. No, she taught me to value the experience of *any* trip for its own sake, to open my mind to color and diversity, to embrace the warmth and hospitality of wonderful people, and to learn to appreciate the fresh perspective that infuses us when faced with scenarios foreign to our everyday existence.

If you want to unbox your mind, then first, unbox yourself. Get on a plane, a train, or a camel. Explore some place you've always wanted to visit, or are even mildly curious about. You'll be amazed at how new horizons open up new possibilities, and at how moving around the world stimulates your confidence, ambition, and creativity. The most surprising thing about travel is that your end destination is seldom the physical place you arrive at, but the personal enrichment you gather along the way.

STOP THE SPIN CYCLE

Drag your thoughts away from your troubles . . .
by the ears, by the heels, or any other way
you can manage it.

Mark Twain,
Author and Humorist

How many of you reading this are wrestling with your own daily mental spin cycle? Problems at work, with your health, at home, in school; a fight with your boss or a disastrous presentation you gave to a client; piles of unpaid bills, spats with the spouse, and stacks of unfinished work; a broken muffler on the car; a letter from your son's teacher—all fight for head space.

The list of everyday stresses is endless, leaving us spinning 'round and 'round, going precisely nowhere. Now what kind of life is that? How the heck can you look forward when you're always going in circles? How can you move purposefully when you're dizzy and disoriented? And how on Earth can you enjoy life when you're all twisted up and wrung out?

Count the times you've gone to bed with an overloaded brain. You know what it feels like: a thousand thoughts swirl around in your head, and your eyes keep poppin' open to stare at the ceiling for hours on end. You toss and turn and flop around, hoping a new position will click off the power to your brain. You're worn out—and yet your brain keeps going.

Busy brains are exhausting. Incessant worry is debilitating, and if you allow it to, will drag you down and render you ineffective. Worry saps your energy and reduces your ability to make smart decisions. A continuous churn of negative thoughts inevitably will eclipse any constructive ones.

Worry is a kind of panic mechanism, a form of self-argument that we use as a means of trying to get back in control of tough situations. *Worry conversations* are unfocused, circular, and rarely productive.

Some folks get hooked on worry; they become addicted to it. But being brain-busy doesn't mean you're making progress. It just means you're using your brain to create circles instead of letting it do what it should be doing at night: *working.*

Our brains, you see, never really shut down. *Nighttime* can be the most productive *brain time* of all. Now I can't pretend to understand the science behind how our gray matter functions (missed that class!), but I do understand the power of those *eureka!* moments that come usually in the early hours of the morning, when a mysterious flash of insight, inspiration, or the solution to a tricky problem jerks you right out of sleep.

And that, my friends, is the wonder of the human brain. Simply plant the seed of your problem before you go to bed, set brain-controls to autopilot, and let the little gray-cell geeks that inhabit your head work their magic while YOU get a decent night's sleep!

Our brains are complex and fertile, packed with brilliance and creativity that can be suffocated or cultivated, dependin' on how we nurture it. And, like any creative genius, your brain'll be a lot more productive if you aren't peering over its shoulder 24/7. So treat your brain like a teenager. Give it a break and get some sleep while it does its own thing. Rather than think of "empty brain time" as wasted time, think of it as an essential time-out called in the second half of the game, so you can catch your breath, regroup, restrategize, and be ready to make that game-winning shot.

Your brain needs a break from worry. Give it some extra breathing room, so it can create those important positive mental pictures. I mean, if you can't switch off from the small stuff, then how are you going to make room for the big picture?

For most people, mental relaxation doesn't come easily. The moment they close their eyes and try to clear some space, an assortment of images rush in and fill the space back up again with distractions. It definitely takes practice to free your mind from the internal, and external, white noise that clutters and interferes. As a kid, I became good at blocking out external disturbances. In our neighborhood, this was an essential skill. The sound of gunfire, sirens, and trouble was usually pretty deafening. You had to tune it out to get any peace at all.

I must confess that I relied on TV to help me do that. My dad and I would sit, side-by-side, like a couple of old men on a park bench, soaking up whatever entertainment came our way. Even as I grew older, I'd keep the TV on when I went to sleep, substituting the sound of movie gunfights for the real battles outside my bedroom window.

To this day, TV has an almost hypnotic effect on me, and though I learned long ago to turn it off at night, you will find me on occasion glued to the set as if even the commercials are Oscar worthy. But in reality, I've moved from the mindlessness of TV toward more creative and constructive ways of relaxing, recharging my brain, and freeing up creative space. The following section offers some of my favorite approaches to relaxing the brain.

The emotional impact of those hours spent on some of the most beautiful golf courses in the country was profound. I stored the images and sensations carefully, and pull them out when my spirit needs restoring:

I'm standing at the top of a grassy hill. It's the end of a long summer day. Dusk is closing in. The air is still except for a rustling in the high branches of the trees and the gently persistent evening birdsong. My footfalls are cushioned by velvety grass. I walk slowly and deliberately, so as not to miss a sound. The breeze whispers, cooling and comforting, soothing and stroking. I feel it wrap around my body and soul; a cloak as real and soft as fine cashmere. In this moment, I find a well of spiritual and mental peace that has eluded me my whole life.—From *Tattoos on My Soul*

REAL TALK I met Trey at my barbershop. He was already an up-and-comer, a young barber in one of the hottest joints in L.A.

He wasn't my barber, but little did I know that Trey was watching me like a hawk—the same way I used to I watch my dad when I was a *shorty*. He said he noticed something different about me; most notably, my smile and positive energy. And, he liked the way I carried myself like a giant.

Now, Trey was off to a good start in life. He was bright, ambitious, and well disciplined. But he was a victim of his own negative spin cycle. Instead of being encouraged by his success, he flipped the script the wrong way and compared himself unfavorably to friends who were more successful. Nevermind that these friends were older and better established. Trey only saw their nice cars, investment properties, and bling. By comparing himself so unfavorably, he had downgraded his own accomplishments to the point of worthlessness, and he was spinning himself into a pit of depression.

One day at the shop, Trey approached me and asked me what my secret was. I told him how I pay myself first, by working out every day, and how I attract success by dressing to impress and greeting the world with a smile and a positive attitude.

Then I turned it back around on him and asked: What did he think was holding him back? Trey said he knew he could probably make some improvements, but he felt like he was always a day late and a dollar short, and always would be no matter what.

Well, I put it to him straight: HE was the one holding himself back! I taught him that Giants are like winning racehorses—they focus on the finish line, not the other horses.

Now, it's important to know where the competition's at, and it's smart to watch other giants and learn from them. But Trey needed to focus on HIMSELF. Do the best that he could do, and do it every day. Forget about what those other guys are doing and worry about yourself, I told him.

Well, Trey took my advice and ran with it like a champ. He started wearing suits to work, exercising more, and greeting everyone with a confident smile. And what do you know? He started attracting more successful clients, more repeat business, and more success. He also scored a new client who helped him achieve his dream of owning real estate. He now owns three properties in Los Angeles and is gearing up to purchase even more.

BRAIN RELAXATION TECHNIQUES

Don't think. Thinking is the enemy of creativity.
It's self-conscious, and anything self-conscious is lousy.
You can't try to do things.
You simply must do things.

Ray Bradbury,
Author

Calm yourself with meditation

The word meditation frightens some people. They think it's some touchy-feely hocus-pocus, some religious ritual, or simply something they're way too busy to do. In a way, meditation is a form of self-hypnosis, but rather than dulling your senses, it makes them clearer and sharper. It's not easy to master, but stick with it and you'll soon begin to appreciate its many benefits.

Here's my *quick-start guide to meditation*:

- Find a quiet place, free from distraction. Shut off the phone, lock the door, and take a moment to get comfortable.

- Place a rug or padded mat on the floor and get settled.

- Sit comfortably (legs crossed or uncrossed) with a straight back, hands in your lap.

- Simply breathe evenly, making sure the breaths are deep and slow.

- Close your eyes and think of a beautiful scene that makes your heart soar. It could be the beach at sunset, the middle of a cool forest, a field of flowers that extends as far as the eye can see. Let waves of well-being wash across your mind.

- Think up a simple, positive phrase and repeat it continuously in time with your breathing. This phrase becomes your *meditation mantra*.

Savvy7

MEDITATION TIPS

Meditation isn't easy. It's a never-ending journey of self-improvement that's often difficult for beginners. Follow these tips to improve your meditation practice.

1 Concentrate. The most difficult part of meditation is quieting the mind. You must empty your mind of thoughts and think about nothing. This requires quite a bit of concentration, as you can imagine.

2 Find a quiet, calming location. In front of the television during the playoffs ain't gonna cut it. You need to be alone and away from distractions.

3 Have intent. You must want to achieve meaningful meditation and the spiritual benefits that go along with it. If you're cynical or trying it just for fun, it's not going to work.

4 Open your heart and mind. For many, meditation is a new experience, and probably a little "granola" for the average American. Accept that you don't know everything, be willing to learn, and you'll get more out of it.

5 Be patient. Meditation, like yoga, can never be perfected, only improved. You won't meditate like a mystical swami on the first day, so have realistic expectations.

6 Sit comfortably with good posture. It's not necessary to cross your limbs, but most pros advise you to place your hands in your lap, palms up.

7 Breathe deeply, concentrating on each inhalation and exhalation.

It's the repetition of affirmations that leads to belief.
And once that belief becomes a deep conviction,
things begin to happen.

Muhammad Ali,
Boxing Heavyweight Champion of the World

Run or power walk

The most effective relaxation technique I know of is to *run* like a gazelle and take joy in the simple experience of *moving*.

Now, running might not sound like relaxation to many of you, but I find physical exertion to be one of the best relaxation techniques of all. It takes my mind away from the everyday details of life and increases my self-awareness. I find the rhythmic pounding of my feet, the sound of my breathing and heartbeat, and the feeling of blood (and life) coursing through my body to be almost hypnotic. I free my mind from consideration of anything that may be worrying me. Instead, I picture in my mind's eye what achieving my goals looks and feels like.

Of course, the added advantage of this approach is that it's not just my brain that becomes fitter, stronger, and more powerful; my body does, too!

Take up yoga

When I finished my first yoga class, I thought my butt had been kicked by Jet Li. My gym regularly offers yoga classes, and I'd peeked in the window a couple of times. One day, on impulse, I decided to try it for myself. After all, it looked pretty easy. If a bunch of light-weights could do it, I sure could; and besides, the teacher hadn't even broken a sweat.

Man, that yoga is something else! I was an exhausted, sweaty mess after that first class and felt like I'd bench-pressed three hundred pounds nonstop for a week. I was also determined there was no way yoga would get the better of me again, and so I began practicing regularly. Yoga, of course, isn't about competitiveness at all; in fact, quite the opposite. But I always preach that you've gotta use whatever motivational techniques work for you, and the challenge of beatin' the game always drives me to greater achievement.

Taking a yoga class in a health club is a good way to get going. Don't become discouraged though, when some young size six balances, bends, and stretches rings around you! Most of us—especially the guys—are pretty competitive and use physical prowess to our advantage whenever we can. Suddenly, we find ourselves in a yoga class where everyone seems to be made of rubber, effortlessly achieving moves that, at first glance, seem impossible (no, I *can't* get my legs to wrap around my neck yet, but I'm working on it). It can be tough on a guy. Oh, and to add insult to injury, you sweat like a dog, too. Yup, getting your ass whupped in a yoga class can be downright humiliating, and your first inclination is to get out of there with your tail between your legs. But don't give up. Stick with it. Yoga is *great* for your body, giving you strength, flexibility, and balance, as well as your mind.

Make music or noise—and get movin'!

Have you lost it? The music that is?

When we were younger, music was part of our lives, part of our very fabric. Music is the soundtrack of our personal stories. It has the ability to stir up a memory, trigger an emotional response, bring a tear to your eye, and, heck, get that body moving like never before!

That's the reason why so many radio channels and TV programs are dedicated to the music we grew up with. Even the kids on *American Idol* sing the "classics" because the music we sang along to as kids is indeed classic. Look, whatever your generation, whether sixties, seventies, eighties, or beyond, and whatever your favorite genre, from rap to country, ska, or pop, I know that when you hear those tunes from way-back-when, your heart lifts, your emotional juices flow, and your body moves of its own accord.

Music was a daily fix when I was a kid. My record collection comprised a somewhat eclectic mix of reggae, soul, Barry White, Frank Sinatra, and just about everything in between. Music made me happy back then, and today my iPod is my most important workout buddy and travel companion. My point? Get yourself an MP3 player, load it up with the music that has defined your life so far, and play it whenever you get the chance: in the car, on the treadmill, out running or walking, at home, or in the office. Inject music back into your life. Clear your mind of clutter and gloom, and use music to reawaken the emotions, optimism, and ambition you had when you were a kid.

Take a road trip

A road trip can be as long or as short as you like. It can be a week-long trek to the opposite coast or an hour winding down country roads. The point of a road trip is to blow out the cobwebs, the worries, the negativity—and just *be*. Hitting the road taps our sense of adventure. The possibilities stretch farther than the eye can see. Often when our multi-tasking mind has nothing more to do than keep the car on the road, it feels free to explore lanes of ideas that can *astound* us.

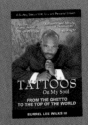

As usual we'd drive, not fly. Having a passion for things European—especially cars and women—I continued to favor Mercedes. These sleek, smooth, reliable workhorses were a triumph of design and performance. We ate up the miles. [My buddy Godfather] would drive, and I'd doze or watch the scenery slip by, mile after mile. These trips were both stimulating and soothing. Sometimes my mind would be all fired up, buzzing with plans and electricity, but mostly I emptied it of all things superfluous and let the world shimmy by, to the rhythm of tires on tarmac.

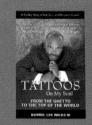

We spent most of the winter months in Miami and Orlando, avoiding the bitter Chicago winters. Indiana and Minneapolis were our springtime destinations, and now and again we'd make a West Coast run. Most people's *eyes* would water at the prospect of forty-plus hours of freeway stretching ahead of them, but our *mouths* did!

I understand why road trips are a great American tradition. This is one heck of a *big* country, and a beautiful one. The chase for the horizon is intoxicating: the sense of freedom and promise and the implicit sense of *possibility,* yet-to-be-defined, but limitless. It's heady stuff. I spent the hours mulling over the past and trying to imagine what a different kind of future could look like.
—From *Tattoos on My Soul*

YA GOTTA DO IT

FREE YOUR MIND

Having difficulties living in the moment? Perhaps you've lost track of reasons to be thankful for today. Right now, write down three things you're thankful for—TODAY. Maybe you had a special moment with a child, or maybe you rolled through all green lights on the drive to work. Or, maybe you got to drive to work, while many other people had to walk or take the bus. Keep your list handy and refer to it throughout the day. Turn your mind around, and you'll turn your life around.

8

STAY AWAY FROM POISONOUS PEOPLE

*Keep away from people
who try to belittle your ambitions.
Small people always do that,
but the really great make you feel
that you, too, can become great.*

Mark Twain,
Author and Humorist

People are either *Givers* or *Takers*: a simple but effective classification. No room for gray. And when I talk about giving and taking, I'm not just referring to people who borrow or lend money. No, I'm talking about *emotional* giving and taking.

You know the people I'm talking about. Takers only want to be around you as long as you bring value to them. They scan the room as they talk to you, checking to see who else might be there, just in case they're missing out on something, or *someone*, "better." Takers are always focused on themselves. They can't turn it off.

Now the trick with Takers is they often *dress up as Givers*. They can be confident, entertaining, and generous, too. They seem to know everyone, slapping you on the back, looking you in the eye, and making you feel good for that moment. But beneath the surface is a survivor with few emotional scruples. They are in it only for themselves. Look closely enough, and the Takers will soon give themselves away. Takers will leech off your money, connections, hospitality, and kindness—and still turnaround tomorrow and take your girlfriend! Takers are *takers*—no matter what their currency—and they see everything as fair game.

Try this. Close your eyes for a moment and make a quick scan of all the faces you know so well, family and friends. Imagine them each wearing a T-shirt with a slogan on the front. Would it say "Giver" or "Taker"? You'll be surprised at how easy it is to identify them—and when you've done that, weed out the Takers as fast as you can!

THE TAKER TIP SHEET

It's one thing to help out a friend in need, but oftentimes we allow others to take advantage of our kindness and generosity. The following are seven signs that your friend is a poisonous person (and needs to be cut out of your life):

1 When you need help, poisonous people are nowhere to be found. Or, if they help you out, they expect something in return.

2 Poisonous people steal from you, either by taking material objects, credit for work, or the affections of another person. They borrow valuable items without asking, then when you insist they first ask permission, or ask them to return the object, they accuse you of being greedy or possessive.

3 The only time you hear from poisonous people is when they are down. You're a friend, not a psychotherapist.

4 Poisonous people brag about their accomplishments, and belittle yours. When you confront the person about the derogatory comments, he or she accuses you of being overly sensitive, unable to take a joke, or unable to handle constructive criticism.

5 Poisonous people are constantly looking over *your* shoulder, scanning the room to see if anyone more "useful" has come into the picture.

6 Poisonous people can only talk about themselves. Count how many times they use "I" in the conversation. You'll be chuckling to yourself before long.

7 After you spend time with a poisonous person, you feel drained, tired, irritable, or depressed.

LOOK OUT FOR THESE TAKERS

*I've always said that in politics, your enemies can't
hurt you, but your friends will kill you.*
Ann Richards,
Governor of Texas

All Takers aren't born equal. Here's a heads up on a few of the different flavors you gotta look out for.

The Oxygen Thieves

Forgive your enemies, but never forget their names.
John F. Kennedy,
U.S. President

I knew a guy once who complained. And complained. And then complained some more. I used to listen and provide positive, actionable advice, but eventually, I gave up. He didn't want advice; he simply wanted attention. Oxygen Thieves are just another form of Taker. Self-absorbed, intense, and malcontented, Oxygen Thieves may not demand anything from you apart from approval, attention, or sympathy, but their self-absorption has to feed off something—and that's likely to be YOU! As their label suggests, they *suck* the oxygen from rooms and the air out of your relationship.

They talk at you, not to you. They don't listen, they don't hear, and they have zero interest in what you have to say. Even when they appear to be paying attention, they're simply waiting for an interruption in your conversational flow so they can jump right back in and talk a little more about themselves. Every sentence begins with "I" and every story ends in "me."

They look you up only when they need something, when their lives are out of kilter, or when they want to tell (or sell) you something.

They love sharing bad news, especially *yours*. Oxygen Thieves aren't usually malicious people, but this kind of deep-rooted selfishness *subtracts* rather than adds to your life. And that's something you can sure do without.

The Bottom Feeders

> *I have no trouble with my enemies.*
> *But my goddamn friends . . . they are the ones that*
> *keep me walking the floor nights.*
>
> **Oscar Levant,**
> **Composer and Comedian**

Now Bottom Feeders are the real losers. The extreme Takers. They'll take, then take a little more, and then just a little more until you're sucked dry. Yup, give a Bottom Feeder an inch and he'll slither into your life and nibble you to death with his *takin'*.

Ironically, most don't even recognize that they're doing you any harm. In fact, they believe that YOU owe THEM. After all, they rationalize, you've got so much more than they do—more money, energy, luck, and connections. It stands to reason you should share it all with them. They feel entitled to a piece of whatever you have.

Larry had a Bottom Feeder problem. His second cousin Brian, who was practically raised with Larry, was leeching him dry. Larry wasn't making a fortune himself, but he had a nice career as a teacher. Brian, on the other hand, only worked seasonal labor jobs—construction in the summer, warehouse work in the winter—and never for more than a couple months at a time.

REAL TALK

About three years ago, Brian's back started giving him trouble, and it became harder and harder for him to do the physical labor. He asked Larry to spot him some cash until he found something easier on his body. So Larry did. After all, what's family for?

Well, that one-time bailout turned into a regular handout; in fact, practically a salary. And don't you know over time, Brian came to *expect* it as an entitlement.

"Thing is, bro," he'd say, "you're more blessed than me. I mean, look at you! Good job, nice family, decent car—all I've got is a couple bucks, a bad back, and more pain than I can handle. It ain't much for a man to wake up to, and it ain't much to ask of you, bro."

But it was a lot to ask. Larry had become his cousin's keeper, shouldering a burden that wasn't his, and with no end in sight. And it wasn't just the money—Brian's mooching was starting to take a toll on Larry's marriage, too.

Know anyone like Brian? A cousin, brother, or friend always on the lookout for financial or emotional handouts? Family can sometimes be the worst of all, especially when they play the kinship card against you.

If you've got a Bottom Feeder in your life, I recommend you take a page from Larry's book. Adamant that he was not going to bale Brian out again, Larry eventually arrived at the tough decision to phase out his donations to him. He sat Brian down, explained that he wasn't prepared to subsidize his living expenses past the next month, but would leverage his connections to help Brian find a job that didn't involve heavy lifting. ("A man's gotta stand on his own two feet," Larry told Brian.) He helped him put a decent résumé together and networked his contacts. Eventually, Brian found a security night-shift position. Is he grateful? *Heck no.* He'll probably lose the job because his attitude is still messed up—now he thinks his *employers* owe him big time. I guess a Taker is always gonna be a Taker!

In the end, we may not get to choose our family, but we always have a choice when it comes to setting personal relationship boundaries. Know your boundaries and know when to say "No!"

The Player Haters

An insincere and evil friend is more to be feared than a wild beast; a wild beast may wound your body, but an evil friend will wound your mind.

Buddha,
Philosopher and Religious Leader

Bottom Feeders may sap your strength and your resources, but they don't tend to be malicious. They're usually too darn lazy! *Player Haters,* on the other hand, have all the energy in the world, most of it negative. These are the guys who like to pour salt on your good news and stop it in its tracks.

When you share good news with them, their smiles are wide but don't quite reach their eyes. They'll "celebrate" your success, slap you on the back, and make the right noises, all the while secretly hoping they'll see you fail. Why? Because if you fail, they won't be *left behind.*

How do you know someone is a Player Hater, when most do such a good job of covering it up, masquerading as friend, partner, or colleague? Well, of course, they'll leave clues, but the best way to tell is how they leave you *feelin'.* When you spend time with a Player Hater, it usually leaves a nasty taste in your mouth. You'll come away feeling vaguely out of sorts, a little uncomfortable and unsettled. In other words, *their negativity rubs off on you.* Give it long enough, though, and all Player Haters eventually show their true colors.

Stacy couldn't quite put a finger on it, but there was something wrong with her relationship with her husband, Kevin. Seems like all they ever did anymore was fight. Kevin was always working late, coming home well after dinner, and he was exhausted and grouchy, too. He refused to talk about it, which left Stacy feeling hurt and isolated, and since he wasn't around much, it gave Stacy lots of time to stew about it.

Thank goodness for Stacy's neighbor, Renee. It was Renee who figured out that Kevin wasn't working late—he was playin' around with another woman. According to Renee, all men were cheating, shallow, selfish bastards who wouldn't think twice about ditching their wives for someone younger and prettier. Renee knew what she was talking about first hand, too. After all, it had happened to her. Renee insisted all men were dogs, and the only way a woman could fight back was by biting first, biting hard, and biting where it hurt the most.

No, not there. The wallet.

So, Stacy made an appointment with a divorce lawyer and got ready to really stick it to Kevin. She sat Kevin down and laid down the law: she was divorcing his no-good, lying behind; and not only that, he was going to PAY.

Except Stacy missed one important fact: Kevin wasn't cheating at all. He really *was* working late, and it wasn't to get ahead—it was to keep his head above water. A big business deal he'd put together had fallen through, and he was fighting for his job. It turned out to be a losing fight because he'd been let go a few

REAL TALK

days earlier. He'd been goin' crazy, trying to figure a way to break the news to Stacy.

Now true, Kevin should have confided in Stacy much earlier, and Stacy should have trusted Kevin. But let's get real: things wouldn't have blown up like that if Renee, the poisonous Player Hater, hadn't intervened and tried to get Stacy to join her miserable man hater's club.

Always remember: misery LOVES company.

One final and alternative thought on this subject: If there weren't Player Haters, there wouldn't be Players. At the end of the day, despite their worst intentions, negative people only serve to make us stronger, fitter, and more successful.

You see, there are two kind of people in the world today
We have, the playaz, and we have, the playa haters
Please don't hate me because I'm beautiful baby.

The Notorious B.I.G.,
from the song "Playa Hater"

DON'T BE A BLAME GAMER

People are always blaming their circumstances for what they are. I don't believe in circumstances. The people who get on in this world are the people who get up and look for the circumstances they want, and, if they can't find them, make them.

George Bernard Shaw,
Nobel Prize-Winning Author and Playwright

Ray swore it was his wife's fault. If she hadn't nagged him into investing in that real estate deal in Costa Rica, he wouldn't have lost all that money.

Louis blamed his brother. He was such a loser, and he'd dragged Doug along with him when he hit those casinos. Now they were both knee-deep in a financial black hole.

Angela knew it was all her husband's doing. He was useless: had no focus, no direction, and now no job. If only he could've gotten his act together, then they would've been fine.

Blame. Blame. Blame.

Why, when things go wrong, do we so often point the finger at someone else? And when it's not your mother, your boss, or your best friend, it's the politicians, or the weather, or the evil corporations that make you lose your money, trip over a crack in the sidewalk and break a leg, get fat, burn yourself with coffee that's too hot, or fill your lungs with cancer-causing smoke. Someone else is always to blame. Yup, "They" are out to get you.

If you're a *Blame Gamer,* you may not know who "They" are by name, but you are adamant that "They" exist. "They" stopped you from getting the best education, blocked your promotion, or made you look stupid in that really important meeting last week. "They" swiped the woman (or guy) you were crazy about while your head was turned, just for a moment. "They" teased and bullied you when you were a *shorty,* leaving you with so many chips on your shoulders you're walkin' crooked. "They" weighted the deck against you, making sure you'd never get ahead in life.

Blame, blame, blame.

The thing is that 90 percent of the time, the illusive "They" are nothing more than figments of our imaginations, existing because we make them real. We breathe life into these characters, turning them into the bogeymen who rule our fates. And we do it because blaming *someone else* is a great way to avoid blaming *ourselves*.

Don't get me wrong. There are mean-spirited, small-minded folks out there. But the reality is, these folks only get their power from us. When we allow them to suck us into their small-minded, jealous little worlds; when we start finger-pointing and blaming; when we stop taking responsibility for our own lives, our own successes—and yes, our own failures—that's when we give negativity its power.

> *If you could kick the person in the pants responsible for most of your trouble, you wouldn't sit for a month.*
>
> **Unknown**

You've got to stop finding all kinds of excuses for why you *won't* succeed, and start finding the reasons for why you *will*. In doing so, you'll discover one of the most fundamental drivers of personal success is personal accountability.

In short, the buck stops with you. Don't be a Blame Gamer.

Tom's Story (Part 1)

REAL TALK

Tom is a classic example of a man stuck in the blame game. Once a successful TV actor, now Tom is in his mid-thirties and trying hard to recapture those glory days. Problem is, Tom's game was no longer happenin', and while the world had moved on, he hadn't.

With every role that passed him over, he grew more angry and frustrated. See, Tom believed his past success should have guaranteed him a future. After all, he had been a star! Yes, Tom had a strong sense of entitlement, and when he didn't get what he felt was his, he looked around for someone to point the finger at. His favorite target was the entire entertainment industry, where "only the friends and relatives of directors got any work," Tom said. As time passed, Tom grew increasingly bitter and even paranoid, convinced that folks were out to ruin his career.

Yeah, you could say Tom was a real pro at the blame game. And not once did he stop to consider the facts: Tom did have talent, but he was operating in a horribly competitive marketplace. TV comedy was his specialty, but he'd been off the scene for more than a decade. A whole new generation of actors had come along, and even they were struggling thanks to the popularity of reality TV shows. Refusing to accept the obvious, Tom instead chose to live in the past.

As he sat around the house, stressing about making the rent, Tom turned to food for comfort. At least there was one thing he could always count on: Popeye's chicken and biscuits. Man, that Popeye's was good—and cheap, too. He stopped going to auditions and spent his days watching reruns of his old shows, with his loyal eight-piece family meal by his side.

Before he knew it, Tom was so fat, unhealthy, and lethargic, he couldn't get an acting gig even if he tried.

We'll come back to Tom's story later . . .

So stay away from the Bottom Feeders, Player Haters, and Oxygen Thieves—*Takers all*—even if they're related to you! Find people who share your goals, will celebrate your successes, and will lift you up on their shoulders, not drag you into the mud. Befriend people who'll be there to encourage you when you need it, not compete with you. Surround yourself with happy, successful, and positive people. Choose to be around Givers who inspire you to give and role models who encourage you to be strong. Never become a Blame Gamer.

Remember: fly with eagles, don't hop with the sparrows, and avoid poisonous people at all costs!

YA GOTTA DO IT

STAY AWAY FROM POISONOUS PEOPLE

Face it. As you read this chapter, you thought of a few people in your life, didn't you? They are holding you back, eating away at you like a cancerous tumor. If you sincerely want to succeed, you must cut at least one poisonous person out, and you must do it today. Poisonous people are toxic, and they make you sick. You are a strong, healthy person. Debate over!

Part3

Burrel's Seven Streetwise Strategies

Here are the tried-and-true success strategies I use every day. These strategies are all you need to drive your transformation from wannabe to winner. Try a few and see what a difference they can make in your life.

9

STREETWISE STRATEGY #1: BECOME A MIND JEDI!

All men dream, but not equally.
Those who dream by night
in the dusty recesses of their minds,
wake in the day to find that it was
vanity, but the dreamers of the day are
dangerous men, for they may act on
their dreams with open eyes,
to make them possible.

Thomas E. Lawrence,
a.k.a. Lawrence of Arabia

Without leaps of imagination, or dreaming,
we lose the excitement of possibilities.
Dreaming, after all, is a form of planning.
Gloria Steinem,
Journalist and Women's Rights Advocate

How many times when you were younger were you told to *quit day-dreamin'* and get back down to Earth? How often did you get yanked out of some nice fantasy, back to the here and now, to concentrate on the things that supposedly *really mattered*, such as algebra, spelling, or helping out with the chores? I'm not saying math and spelling and chores aren't important, because they are. But it strikes me as odd that, as kids, we have the daydreamin' knocked out of us pretty young so that we can focus our minds and energy on *real life*.

The irony is, in my experience, that real life is lived most fully by those who dare to dream, and most importantly, by those who dare to dream with their "eyes open." In fact, real life is the sum of our dreams, and the daydreamers who dare to *see the invisible in order to make the impossible happen* will potentially have the richest lives. Success is a state of mind. I believe, beyond a shadow of a doubt, it can be achieved by harnessing the limitless mind power with which we've all been blessed.

One of the biggest things I've learned over the years
is that "you are what you think."
You are able to create your own destiny simply
by the things you think about.
If your expectancy is to fail,
then that is what you will probably do.
If, however, you have absolute confidence that
you are going to succeed, then whatever "ups and
downs" you experience, you will interpret them
as steppingstones . . . to your eventual success.
Malcolm Harvey,
Entrepreneur

But can dreamin' really change anything? Well, when I was a kid, I dreamed a lot. I'd imagine myself successful. I'd *see, feel, and taste* what it would be like. It was so real in my mind, as to be almost indivisible from the truth. You see, the raw power of imagination is incalculable. Think of it this way: Imagination is a mental dress rehearsal for the real thing. If you practice often enough, you'll soon be so familiar with success, even your mind won't be able to tell the difference!

DREAMING ON THE DRIVE

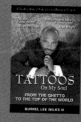

Like so many other Chicago black kids, I frequently daydreamed my way down the section of Lake Shore Drive that converges so sweetly with downtown Chicago. It was a favorite pastime. Cruising along with the top down and a couple of buddies on warm summer nights. We'd crank up the decibels until Frank Sinatra or Michael Franks was blasting from the speakers with enough force to lift us off the road. Puffing on a joint, we'd meander up and down that beautiful stretch of highway, admiring the city's dramatic profile.

I loved the brick and stucco, white-glove buildings that formed one boundary of the S-Curve, a sweeping arc of road stretching from North Lake Shore to East. These dignified and stately apartments dominated the skyline, standing shoulder to shoulder, their banks of bright, unblinking eyes reflected on a patent leather lake. This neighborhood was home to some *serious* old money.

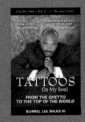

We'd stop, get out, and sit down with our backs to the water, leaning back far enough to be able to gaze upwards without cricking our necks. Picking out the penthouses, we'd imagine what it would be like to live in one of those *palaces in the sky.*

When those big, high-ceiling apartments were lit up from the inside, you might catch a glimpse of a flickering TV screen, the movement of people, or the glitter of a majestic glass chandelier. We wove stories by the dozen and dreamed out loud. What great parties we'd throw, and what fine hosts we'd be! What beautiful women we'd have on our arms, how much Crystal champagne we'd drink, and how *everyone* would look at us with envy.

It took me years to understand that those mind-pictures I painted hadn't really been about *owning* an apartment on Lake Shore Drive at all. Rather those balmy, storytelling evenings had reflected a deep hankering to be the *kind of man* who inhabited one of those elegant, status-conscious buildings. I yearned to be a man of stature and substance, respected and accepted by other powerful people.

Even as a young gang chief, I aspired to be more than Buddy Burrel, leader on my block. I wanted to be a *leader of men.* Unable to articulate it in words, I dreamed it instead.
—From *Tattoos on My Soul*

Today, when not in L.A. or New York, I live in one of those high-rise apartments on Lake Shore Drive and can spend hours looking out at Lake Michigan, remembering that irrepressible boy and his daydreams that came to life.

> *Twenty years from now, you will be more disappointed*
> *by the things that you didn't do*
> *than by the ones you did do.*
> *So throw off the bowlines.*
> *Sail away from the safe harbor.*
> *Catch the trade winds in your sails.*
> *Explore. Dream. Discover.*

Mark Twain,
Author and Humorist

IMAGINE YOURSELF SUCCESSFUL

I am enough of an artist to draw freely upon my
imagination. Imagination is more important
than knowledge. Knowledge is limited.
Imagination encircles the world.

Albert Einstein,
Nobel Prize-Winning Theoretical Physicist

Those of us who spend time in California are fortunate. We have miles and miles of beautiful coastline laid out at our feet, like a long chain of glittering gold and turquoise. With the air currents whipping up tangy, fresh breezes and white-capped waves skittering across the ocean surface, there are few things more glorious than driving along Pacific Coast Highway on a sunny day, top down, music high, soaking it all up—literally *inhaling* life.

Believe it or not, many people have never seen the ocean. In fact, Chicago inner city kids sometimes never even get to see the vast expanse of Lake Michigan, around which Chicago is built. To them, the lake might seem as far away as the ocean. But the ocean represents a different kind of energy. If you haven't stood on the ocean shore on a windy day (or maybe watched the movie *The Perfect Storm*), then it's hard to get a true sense of the raw power of that mass of water.

The ocean is a great metaphor for life. A fathomless reservoir, ebbing and flowing relentlessly, tirelessly; some days warm and gentle, other days fearsome and furious. It generates waves of pure energy that can suck you down, swirl you around, or carry you along for miles and miles, high on their crests. It's your choice. You can decide to drift with the current and see where it takes you; close your eyes and sink like a stone; swim like hell; or, if you're really smart, harness the velocity of those waves and surf like a champion!

It's the same with your imagination. Once you truly understand its power, you'll be carried along on the crest of its waves, a ride as mysterious as it is exhilarating.

104

BURREL'S SEVEN STREETWISE STRATEGIES

Whenever a negative thought concerning your personal power comes to mind, deliberately voice a positive thought to cancel it out.

Dalai Lama,
Spiritual Leader

TIME TO SHOOT SOME "MIND MOVIES"

The soul never thinks without a picture.

Aristotle,

Philosopher

I didn't understand the potency of creating *mind movies* until many years after my first cruise along Lake Shore Drive. That's when I happened upon the work of Dr. Maxwell Maltz, a renowned plastic surgeon turned "self-image psychologist."[1]

In short, Dr. Maltz labeled this power of positive mental imagery *psycho-cybernetics*. His book by the same name is the kind of dusty old paperback you'd find at a garage sale. Popular back in the 1960s, the ideas packed into its small pages have improved millions of lives.

Dr. Maltz's method of creating this "rule book" was interesting, too. You see, he was fascinated by the way people's personalities changed, sometimes drastically, following a cosmetic surgery procedure. In particular, he noticed how people's self-esteem and self-confidence blossomed when they looked in the mirror and saw themselves new and beautiful, and how their self–image changed for the better. It's the kind of thing we see regularly on reality TV shows such as *Extreme Makeover.*

But, even more interesting were the stories of those patients whose personalities *didn't change* after they'd had a makeover. And it was these folks, the ones who continued to feel inadequate and inferior even after their successful nose job, face-lift, or liposuction, that convinced Dr. Maltz corrective surgery was really needed *on the inside, not the outside.*

Now there's a thought!

He concluded that *self-image*, that inner picture we each carry around inside our heads, imprinted deeply in our subconscious, is

---

1. Maxwell Maltz is the author of *Psycho-Cybernetics, A New Way to Get More Living Out of Life* (Pocket Books, 1960) and the *New Psycho-Cybernetics* (Prentice Hall Press, 2002).

really what dictates how confident we are and whether or not we have the ability to become "successful personalities."

Back when I was a shorty, I believed everyone was born with the will and means to be successful, and that we could program ourselves for success if we only knew which buttons to push. And for many people, myself included, that is the case. I've always known that I have the power to be whatever I want to be; though, even as a youth, I realized it would require every ounce of mind power, imagination, hard work, and discipline to get there.

I used to get impatient with guys who didn't have the same highly developed "success-sense" that I did, but over the years I've come to realize that many folks simply aren't born with it—*they have to grow it.* That's when I started to coach the guys around me about the power of positive thinking, and show them different ways to tap into their own inner force.

I coached them on how to be proud and strong, and taught them the power of self-belief. As I got older and smarter myself, I'd encourage them to get fit and healthy, too, because a strong mind, body, and spirit fit together like a three-legged stool. As your body becomes harder, faster, and fitter, so your mind muscle does, too. Most definitely, I preached *the power of mental visualization.*

Visualization is like shooting a mind movie. Imagine: there you are, relaxing in the backyard of your own beautiful beach house, watching the sun go down over the ocean. You're worn out, but comfortable after a day on the golf course. Drink in hand, the only sounds are the waves breaking below, and the chink of the glasses and plates being laid out on the patio table by your lovely wife.

Nice picture, but still not quite enough.

You see, you must do more than simply *visualize* your goals as though they're promos for an upcoming movie. That might be quite entertaining, and even motivating, but it's not going to help you much. No, you've actually got to *feel your dreams* by projecting yourself right onto center stage! It's not a case of "there you are"; instead, it's a case of "*here* I am" smack-bang in the middle of the story. Your two-dimensional movie trailer is now a 3-D sensory extravaganza. *Now* you're actually standing on the beach, smelling the salty air, feeling the sand between your toes, and enjoying a warm, tropical breeze. Feels great, doesn't it? You can almost taste the salt on your lips and the *realness* of it all.

You see, dreams aren't going to come alive, if you don't *feel* them, *smell* them, and, most importantly, *believe* in them. You've got to get all the way into the picture. Did I say 3-D? Heck, I'm looking for 4-D, 5-D, 20-D!

Mental picturing is so powerful, it seems almost magical, but it's not. It's a natural, powerful, and underutilized tool we all have in our mental arsenals. In fact, it's a strategy athletes have been using for years.

Remember the movie *Caddyshack*, when expert golfer Chevy Chase advises a young up-and-comer to "See the ball; be the ball"? That really is what the greats do. They stand at the free-throw line and mentally see that ball swishing through the net; they feel their muscles performing the act before the ball even leaves their hands. Golfers see the putt going into the hole before they tap the ball. Tennis pros feel the actions of hitting that ace before they toss the ball up to serve.

I always won in my imagination.
I always hit the game-winning shot,
or I hit the free throw.
Or if I missed, there was a lane violation,
and I was given another one.
Mike Krzyzewski,
Duke University Basketball Coach

Now see, when all your energy is focused on these positive mental movies, you're not only *programming* yourself for success-activation, you're also forcing out all the negative stuff that creeps into your head. There's simply no room left for it. Your entire focus is on the *positive.* When you are driven by a clearly visualized end game, there is no brain power left for negative images. In other words, not only do you activate the good energy, but by doing so, you automatically deactivate all the bad energy, too!

BURREL'S SEVEN STREETWISE STRATEGIES

Whatever the mind can conceive and believe,
the mind can achieve.

Napoleon Hill,
Author

I know this mental imagery stuff isn't easy, and you may need some help to learn how to do it. (I've listed some great brain-relaxation techniques in chapter 7.) You might have to meditate or even try professional hypnosis. But once you crack it, it'll be like winning the lottery, because you'll be on the fast-track to success.

STRAIGHTEN UP AND FLY RIGHT

You know, anything I ever heard Burrel talk about,
I saw materialize. I watched it all unfold
just the way he said it would.
Even the things I thought impossible.

Messiah (friend)

I used to be a terrible passenger. A self-reliant guy, I prefer not to place my fate in someone else's hands. I'd usually drive myself rather than accept a lift, even if I had to travel cross-country. I even avoided taking a plane if I could ('course that's all changed now; feels like I spend half my life on planes these days). For years, I was like a cat on a hot tin roof if I had to sit in the backseat with someone else driving or anytime I traveled on an airplane.

I remember this guy, a friend of my cousin's, who'd sometimes shuttle us around Chicago. He had this unfortunate habit of turning around to talk to the guys in the backseat while he was driving, and every time he swiveled, the car would, too! We'd all yell at him, and he'd straighten up fast; but within a minute or two, he'd be back at it. The moment his eyes left the road, we'd start weaving again.

The same thing happens with people. If we don't have a clear destination, keep our eyes on the road and hands firmly on the wheel, then there's little chance we're gonna stay in the right lane.

Even big companies recognize the need for a destination—they call it a *mission statement.* It sort of floats above the chaos of day-to-day business as a map and a beacon, reminding each employee of the core reason why they, and the company, are there in the first place. And don't you know, companies that forget about their mission statements swerve and weave recklessly around the marketplace, just like my cousin's friend.

LAYING IT OUT IN BLACK AND WHITE

The entrepreneur is essentially a visualizer and actualizer. He can visualize something, and when he visualizes it, he sees exactly how to make it happen.

Robert L. Schwartz,
Author

What makes one man a dreamer and another a visionary? What separates the billionaires from the bankrupt, the entrepreneurs from the gamblers, the winners from the wannabes? Why is it our dreams vaporize into thin air when that nasty old alarm clock interrupts us from our great mind movies, and announces it's time to start the ol' daily grind?

Do dreams ever come true? Oh, for sure!

Will dreams ever come true without YOU making them true? Not gonna happen.

You can wish and hope and pray for a miracle all you want, but in the end, we all have to make our own magic. So how do we separate the real, achievable ambitions from never-gonna-happen wishes? How can we be sure that we won't be "tilting at windmills" for the rest of our lives, increasingly disillusioned as disappointment stacks up? How can you become a heat-seeking success missile and not some Ricochet Rabbit hoppin' around from one bright shiny idea to the next?

Converting your dream into *tangible goals* against which you can measure pace and progress is no easy task:

- Where do you start?

- How far out do you look?

- How bold and brave can you afford to be?

Humans respond well to goals, even if the goal is a modest one like getting through to the next paycheck, or making it to the end of the day without falling asleep, or even staying alert through the next hour or two of boring meetings.

One school of thought—the majority opinion—promotes creating tangible, measurable goals and writing them down. Until they are written down, the argument goes, they're nothing more than pipe dreams.

Others say that once you write it down, you risk dumbing down the dream, a trap to be avoided at all costs.

So what should you do? I say be S.M.A.R.T. about it.

EFFECTIVE ACTION PLANNING

Your goal should be out of reach but not out of sight.

Anita DeFrantz,
Olympic Bronze Medalist, Rowing

Set S.M.A.R.T. goals

The concept of S.M.A.R.T. goals is simple to grasp and one of the most widely applied and effective frameworks for goal setting.
S.M.A.R.T. stands for:

- **Specific:** Make sure your objectives are *detailed.*

- **Measurable:** Be able to *measure* whether you're meeting your goals or not.

- **Achievable:** Are your goals *attainable?*

- **Realistic:** Do you have the *resources* to achieve your goals?

- **Time:** What is your *time frame* and *key milestones?*

Make sure all your goals are S.M.A.R.T. goals, and you'll increase your chances for success. But, be wary of falling into these traps:

Don't dumb 'em down

When people write down their goals, its human nature to dumb them down—to build in a little *slack* for ourselves. Most people consistently under-rate themselves and set the bar too low. First, we allow our limited perceptions of *ourselves* to limit what we believe we can *achieve.* "I can't possibly do that, we say. Better stick with something more sensible and safe." So we begin the process of *reducing our aspirations.*

Don't be afraid to set visionary goals—after all, your goals should be a reflection of your dreams and can be as big as your imagination allows. Size doesn't matter. Why? Because you're going to refine your goals until they are S.M.A.R.T. goals and because you can break your goals down into bite-size pieces. (We'll talk about "Bite-size or King-size" in a bit.)

Cut out the escape clauses

When our goals are laid out on paper, frankly, it scares the crap out of us, because, let's be honest, it means we're committing *to doing something!* We don't want to fail—that would be just another disappointment—so we build in all kinds of escape clauses, just in case. If you have an escape clause in your goal, it indicates you aren't committed to that goal. Don't set yourself up for failure like these folks:

- "Yes, I'll have made a million in real-estate equity within five years, and then double it every couple of years after that. Well, five years from when I make my first big purchase anyway, which may not be for quite some time, the market being what it is . . ."

- "Yes, I'll retire with my own boat by the time I'm fifty . . . unless, of course, I'm really loving my job, in which case I may keep working until I'm sixty."

- "Yes, I'll open my own business by January 1, in two years time . . . unless, of course, I get that promotion I've been angling for, in which case I may stick with the corporate world for a while."

Build on your own reality

Other people don't know you. Only YOU know how your internal "wiring" really works. You may have to adjust your course a few times, revise your goals, and refocus your efforts, but never mentally block yourself in and never pigeon-hole yourself to the point where you accept failure as an outcome.

Derek thought he had his life set: he was driven, focused, and had a degree in business administration. All his life he had been told he was a left-brained, analytical type; a numbers guy, who used logical, linear thinking—definitely NOT a creative type.

Though he loved to write creatively, he never took it seriously. After all, he'd been told by so many people that just wasn't "him," and how could all those people be wrong? So Derek did what he was told and pursued a career in operational work, specializing in compliance and procedures.

But he wasn't happy. Instead, he was miserable, stressed out, and exhausted from forcing himself to do work he didn't enjoy. So, I encouraged him to write a screenplay. To say he was reluctant would be an understatement. Dude was flat out pissed off at me for forcing him outside his comfort zone and for making him challenge himself in new and unexpected ways.

It took him a year to get over it and get to crackin'. We agreed to a firm goal that he would complete the writing within six months. And man, was that screenplay on time! It was even good enough to catch the eyes of a few real industry players. Today Derek is a freelance copywriter and lovin' every minute of it. He's got mountains of self-esteem and plenty of ideas that utilize his creative talents and will, very soon, have him on the track to wealth.

BITE-SIZE OR KING-SIZE ACTION?

*A thought which does not result in an action is
nothing much, and an action which does not proceed
from a thought is nothing at all.*

**Georges Bernanos,
Novelist and Essayist**

You cannot drive success without taking action. Everyone's heard that "the road to Hell is paved with good intentions." Well, unfortunately, the road to success isn't. You can't realize goals—no matter how beautifully laid out—without taking action. The question is: how much action is needed?

Some folks confuse movement with action. You'd probably be as surprised as I was at first, to learn about the huge number of people who buy self-help programs and books, subscribe to self-improvement courses, and join health clubs—sometimes spending hundreds, even thousands, of dollars—and then don't even open the package or cross the threshold! Or, maybe not. Perhaps you're one of these same people!

In conversations with direct marketers, I've been told that for some self-help programs, less than 50 percent of buyers even unwrap their purchases—but they feel better anyway, simply for having taken some kind of positive action. In fact, many direct marketers make a lot of money from human *apathy*. Ever wonder about those "money-back" guarantees? Most marketers know that folks, in general, are too lazy to bother to send anything back. In fact, they bank on it.

Bite-size pieces

One of the best ways to take action on your goals is to break your goals down into bite-size pieces or baby steps. You don't have to take giant leaps. Reaching your goals is like climbing stairs, if you patiently place one foot in front of the other, steady and constant, you'll eventually arrive at the top. I've got a lot of respect for this "one-day-at-a-time" approach to success. I like it because it's real, sustainable, delivers solid results, and, through repetition, helps you develop new positive habits. Once these healthy habits become engrained in your everyday behaviors, progress becomes a way of life.

Steady, persistent progress also means you're less likely to get discouraged—because even when you hit obstacles you keep plowing forward, one step at a time. Like water on stone—*drip, drip, drip*—you will eventually carve a path.

King-size change

BUT, paradoxically, to get the best results we need to be *impatient,* too. We must always cultivate a sense of great urgency. Remember, we only have limited time to strive, thrive, and achieve, and in this crazy, fast-moving, dog-eat-dog world, having endless patience and being too easy on ourselves is not *always* a virtue!

REAL TALK

Glen was no go-getter. He was more of a go-with-the-flow kind of guy. Although he had a sales job, it was pretty undemanding: he had his regular customers who gave him steady business, and that was enough for him. He wasn't a big spender and lived comfortably on the money he made. He even had a nice-sized savings account. Really, his only guilty pleasure was trout fishing. He'd traveled all across the country to fish in rivers famous for their trout. He had a nice, routine life, and that's just the way he liked it.

But we both know that's not the end of the story. Life is never that simple. Glen's company got bought out, and he didn't make the cut when the layoffs hit his department. At first, he wasn't too worried. He'd just live off his savings for a while and get another job like his last one. But that job never came, and when the money started running out, he started to panic. He realized he was just an average, middle-aged guy with no marketable skills, few job prospects, and absolutely no clue how he was going to support himself.

He spent a lot of time online, looking for a new job, but also joining online communities dedicated to fishing. Soon, he recognized there was an opportunity to turn his hobby into a real, profitable business. He launched a number of niche fishing Web sites and began selling hard-to-find fishing supplies and insider information regarding the best fishing spots in the country. He charged $20 per month for membership to a fishing club, in which he and other members shared the best "insider information" around. His next step is to organize his own fishing tours, taking fellow fishing hobbyists to his favorite spots. Now, Glen isn't exactly ballin' with his fishing biz, at least not yet. But he has real passion for his work and is building a reputation in the fishing world as a real player!

Many of the most famous motivators and life coaches out there—people like Zig Ziglar and Anthony Robbins—are advocates of *radical change*. Without radical change, they suggest, real transformation is tough to achieve. This was certainly true in Glen's case, where it took losing his job to move him out of his rut and unlock his potential.

Throughout my life, although I've worked consistently toward my goals, real advancement has come whenever I've made a real, profound, fundamental *shift* in my life.

I call this *king-size change!*

Of course, it was tough for me to extract myself from my life as a gangster. It was hard to claw my way out of the ghetto and into a more positive environment. But when I upped the stakes and physically moved myself into the suburbs, my transformation accelerated dramatically. Moving from the 'hood was certainly a king-size change. Okay, I wasn't yet in the right place success-wise and I still had a long furrow to plow, but only by breaking with the old, could I make room for the new.

A Friend's Story

REAL TALK

"It was nearly twenty years ago now, and I was in a really bad situation. Living in London, I was having a tough time at work and still recovering from the loss of my mother a couple of years earlier. When the company I worked for downsized and cut me loose, it shouldn't have come as a shock, but it did. All in all, it was a devastatingly bad time for me, and I couldn't see any light at the end of the tunnel. The job market was flat. I was broke, isolated, depressed, and if it hadn't been for my wonderful family, I don't know what I would have done.

"In the end, what I did do was quite drastic. I got on an airplane with a round-the-world ticket clutched in my hand and set off—job hunting! I financed the trip by remortgaging my home, which I then leased out. It was a big risk. I was over-leveraged. If I didn't find a job, I'd come back to a mountain of debt and the same poor job prospects. But I didn't go back. Ever. I traveled the world to Africa, Mauritius, Singapore, Malaysia, Thailand, Hong Kong, and China. I got robbed along the way but muddled through. I met some wonderful, warm, generous people who helped me along, and I also got a job. A great one. I stayed in Asia for almost ten years, and that trip radically and dramatically changed my life forever."

So incremental action doesn't always cut it. Sometimes you have to embrace king-size change—take enough risk to allow the *dream* to lead the *reality* and let hope and optimism drive the end game.

Bite off more than you can chew, then chew it.

Ella Williams,
Entrepreneur

Savvy**7**

GOAL-SETTING TIPS

We all know we should have goals, but where do you start? Sometimes it's hard to stand back and take an objective look at yourself. So here's a thought: ask a friend or family member to work through these tips with you, and then do the same for them.

1 **Understand where you are today. Try to identify choices and behaviors, past and present, which brought you here. Understand where you want to be in the future. Assume everything is possible.**

2 **Convert your vision into a simple promise to yourself. For example: "I will retire on my fiftieth birthday to a house by the ocean, with enough money saved to live a comfortable, worry-free lifestyle."**

3 **Clear some head space and spend some quality time imagineering, until you can see, feel, and taste your dream.**

4 **Write down everything you can think of that will help you achieve your promise to yourself. Let the ideas free-flow. Don't constrain yourself.**

5 **Prioritize the things you can act on immediately, the larger steps you must build up to, and identify at least one king-size action!**

Savvy7

6 Build a storyline, or a *pathway of action,* all the way to your end goal and overlay key milestones and timelines.

7 Pick three things you will do in the next day, the next week, and the next month. In other words, *get started.*

YA GOTTA DO IT

BECOME A MIND JEDI!

If you're really serious about change, set three goals for yourself right now: one thing you will accomplish today, one thing you will accomplish this week, and one thing you will accomplish this month. Big or little, it's up to you: find a new job or clean out your messy car. Make sure you write your goals down and post them in a place you'll see them frequently, like on your computer monitor at work, or on the refrigerator at home. Cross them off as you complete them, to give yourself a feeling of accomplishment and the motivation to move on to bigger goals!

10

STREETWISE STRATEGY #2: HUSTLE WITH HEART

Everything comes to him who hustles while he waits.

Thomas A. Edison,
Inventor

ARE YOU A "WORKER" OR A "HUSTLER"?

*What you lack in talent can be made up with desire,
hustle, and giving 110 percent all the time.*

**Don Zimmer,
Major League Baseball Coach**

I used to say that a worker could never be a hustler, and a hustler could never be a worker. These days I have a different perspective. I believe, now, that a hustler must add substance to his game, while a worker, with his nose always to the grindstone, has gotta add some sizzle! In the end, we all need to add a pinch of hustle to our lives.

Before we go further, let's discuss the concept of *hustling*. For many folks, there's something slightly off-color about the idea of hustling. It conjures up negative images and feels sort of dirty.

The dictionary doesn't do much to dispel that notion either. Here are a few standard definitions:

- "To go somewhere or do something fast or hurriedly"

- "To engage in small-time crimes, for example, petty theft"

- "To solicit customers in shady or illegal deals"

I can see why none of these is appealing. But what about this one:

- "To play a sport with great aggressiveness, intensity, and concentration"

Now we're making progress. So what if we substitute life for sport? A couple more tweaks, and now you have my own unique, Streetwise definition of hustling:

- "To play the game of life with focus, intensity, and heart"

You see, there's good hustle and bad hustle. *Bad hustle* is when you're all about the game. Glitzy, selfish, slick, and shallow, bad hustlers bring no value to the table. They're all about short-term wins and lining their own pockets, and frankly, they don't give a damn how they do it. There's no future for these guys.

But good hustle, *hustling with heart,* is all about injecting urgency, determination, and passion into your game, as you take it up to a whole new level. The sizzle is evident, but so too are the results.

So what makes me a good hustler?

Well, I live my life with a great sense of urgency. I know I don't have a moment to waste, so I relish every one of them. I live each moment to the fullest—which for me means never waiting for good fortune to happen to me, but going out and hunting it down. I'm fearless and unafraid to cross lines, burst through doors, push myself out of my comfort zone, and chase down opportunity. I embrace challenge and risk. I redefine my boundaries every single day. And I'm never afraid to ask for something. It amazes me how so few people know how to ask for what they want or need. Don't ask and you won't get; it's as simple as that.

Most important of all: *I never give up.* The essence of a true hustler is that he never, ever, admits defeat. Defeat isn't a word that's in his vocabulary. A set-back is just a new opportunity. A bad day is just the prelude to a good one. A boo is simply a cheer in disguise. Bad times just make the good ones all the sweeter.

Remember, there's nothing wrong with adding some hustle to your game, so long as it's the right kind of hustle: hustle with heart.

> *I never got into it for the music.*
> *I got into it for the business.*
>
> **Curtis "50 Cent" Jackson,**
> **Entertainer**

Savvy 7

SHOULD YOU BE YOUR OWN BOSS?

Is self-employment for you? Most self-made millionaires are entrepreneurs. Ask yourself these seven important questions to determine whether or not you're suited for being your own boss. The more "yes" answers, the more likely you'll make it on your own.

1 Do you find something else to do when you finish your work early?

2 Can you make quick decisions under pressure?

3 Are you willing to lower your standard of living and/or live off your savings for awhile in order to make your dream happen? Most small businesses don't turn a profit the first two or three years.

4 Are you your own best motivator? Well organized and focused?

5 Do you leave the office after the work is done, instead of 5 p.m. on the dot?

6 Starting projects on your own initiative is one thing, but do you also finish them? Follow-through is an essential quality for the self-employed.

7 Most important of all, do you have a great business idea, backed up by a realistic business plan, and enough persistence to make it real?

I am a businessman.
This is what I do each and every day.
I love it. I love coming to work.
I never have a bad day.

Magic Johnson,
NBA Basketball Legend

126

HUSTLING GETS RESULTS!

Things may come to those who wait, but only the things left by those who hustle.

Abraham Lincoln,
U.S. President

We all hustle to one degree or another, but most people don't recognize it for what it is. "Of course, I don't know how to hustle!" they'd say if confronted with the question. "What kind of a person do you think I am?"

Take Marcus. During the course of a single day, he jostled his way to the front of a line, haggled for a discount price on a second-hand car, persuaded the nice lady at the deli to throw in an extra slice of honey-baked ham at no charge, and borrowed a few bucks off a friend. Now, to my mind, that's a pretty darn good day's hustling!

Hustling is, after all, simply a way of getting things done, of getting what you need, and asking for what you want. It requires displacing the old, timid you with a more assertive, direct, and, yes, honest you.

But few people are good at hustling with heart. As we said earlier, the folks who are *natural* hustlers usually rely too much on the *play,* and the guys who aren't naturals, the workers, have to overcome their natural inhibitions. They may try a play now and then, but in truth, game playing seldom sits easily on square shoulders, and as often as not, will fail. Hustlers are natural-born extroverts and actors, but worker bees are often more reserved.

The cover-your-butt mentality of the workplace will get you only so far. The follow-your-gut mentality of the entrepreneur has the potential to take you anywhere you want to go or run you right out of business— but it's a whole lot more fun, don't you think?

Bill Rancic,
***The Apprentice* Winner**

A while ago I attended a major book convention in Washington, and, man, was that an eye-opener! If you think the world of books is a polite, civilized, academic kind of place, I have to tell you, you couldn't be more wrong. Book publishing has to be one of the *toughest* businesses I've come across. Of course, there's intellectual snobbery involved and an old-boys' network, but this doesn't deter thousands of aspiring writers—*the small guys*—from investing time, emotion, and even life savings in the dream.

REAL TALK

I don't know why I thought it would be any different at a book convention, but, turns out, the book biz is nothing but one big hustle. The last time I saw that many hustlers in one place, I was a kid on Chicago's rough West Side. Just like on the street corner, there were guys hustling to get noticed, hustling to make a deal, hustling to move their product, hustling to find other people to move their product, hustling to get a reputation—you name it! There were even guys lugging around heavy sacks of free books they'd hustled right out of those vendor's booths—and they were headed straight home to hustle them on eBay! Everybody had one hustle or another at that show.

Except those who didn't.

These were *the workers*—guys who wouldn't know a hustle if it hit them upside the head. And believe it or not, there were quite a few of them, all bright and optimistic, hoping that they would be "discovered" in the crowd and awarded multimillion-dollar deals. These were the one-book authors, who spent their life savings self-printing 150 copies of their life's work. Problem was, nobody was interested in discovering them, except maybe the players—and the only thing the players cared about was how to make a buck or two off their naiveté!

So the message is pretty clear.

We've ALL got to mix in a little hustle with our work if we want to be successful. I said it up-front and I'll say it again: you're already in the game. It's called LIFE, and you don't have the luxury of sitting it out. You may not like the hand you've been dealt, but like it or not, you're a player, so you better start playing to win. Now here's where I'm gonna give you a chance to improve your hand with some serious Streetwise advantage. You see, I've compiled something very special for you, and I've called it: *The Hustle with Heart Handbook.*

Don't skim over this next section, because these *twelve essential rules* will help you start to get the results you deserve.

THE
HUSTLE
WITH HEART
HANDBOOK

12 Easy Rules To Get The Results You Want

BURREL'S SEVEN STREETWISE STRATEGIES

1 Know your ABC's (always be closin')

Know your ABC's. In other words, *always be closin'*. No, this doesn't mean you've gotta try and sell something every time you speak to another person (except yourself, of course—you should always have an eye on *that* sale), but it does mean that you should never miss the opportunity to make your mark.

Remember, every single contact is a chance to make something good happen. Instead of just shaking hands and moving on, take a moment to make an impression on each person you meet. It doesn't take much: a firm handshake, a friendly remark, direct eye contact, remembering a name, taking a moment longer than absolutely required. Small investment. BIG return.

Business or personal, every *connection point* should become a *progress point*, every conversation an opportunity to develop your *Personal Power Brand* (more on this in chapter 13), and every new exposure an excuse to build your visibility and reputation. Working your connections isn't cynical; it's shrewd.

2 Keep stickin' and movin'

Once you understand how to turn connection points into progress points, you'll understand the value of nurturing, extending, and growing your personal connections network. You can never know *too many* people, because you never know where your next break will come from.

A first-rate network is priceless. Naturally enough, winners recognize this and make networking a part of their daily routine. They understand two important things: first, that there's plenty of opportunity to go around if you know where to find it. And second, that though this is a *trade*, or an *exchange*, they must invest *without* expectations of an immediate return. They know that when the return does come, it'll be ten-, twenty- or a hundred-fold the initial investment. This is called the *pay it forward* approach to networking.

So don't think for a minute that golf outings, chamber of commerce functions, lunches, and "just touching base" chats are simply pleasant social diversions. No, sir! This is how hardcore networking works and, by the way, it's something that men are *way* better at than women. That's no criticism of women, but it is a disadvantage. Networking is something boys are raised to do from birth, but most women must learn later in life. So, if you want to get on in the world, you've gotta invest time, energy, and effort in building your own power network.

How? Well, for years I traveled back and forth across the U.S. for work and pleasure, criss-crossing this country, and sometimes others, from coast to coast. Today it doesn't matter where I am: Miami, Chicago, Washington, New York, L.A., or points in between, you can be pretty certain that I'll find someone I know, or who knows of me, who will show me around and open some doors.

These days, of course, you don't have to move out of your home to become a consummate power networker. I spend countless hours on my phone, tuning in with the hundreds of guys I've met through the years and making sure all the links in my network are "oiled." But it's the digital revolution that has truly put the world at our fingertips. Online network communities are growing faster than weeds, and though I don't believe there's a real substitute for face-to-face connection, if you don't have the time to get out and about, or the social skills or confidence to network in person, or if you just don't know where to begin, then check out the virtual world.

Social and professional networks like LinkedIn or MySpace are amazing. Without moving from your chair, you can meet literally millions of people. Of course, some will be flakes, but you'll know how to sift them out easily enough, by applying some of the fundamentals of my Streetwise Strategies. In any case, you can be pretty sure there is a virtual community out there, somewhere, focused on the same social, business, or hobby interests as you. *Let your fingers do the walkin' and the talkin'!* Today, in this amazing digitally distributed world, there's no reason on Earth to be alone, unsupported, or unconnected.

3 Understand the power of "catering"

Okay, so you've made the connection, now you want to make sure you exploit it as effectively as possible (in a positive sense). If you're going to extract the most from your connections, then you must understand the power of *catering*.

Remember I mentioned earlier that whatever you put in, you'll eventually get out ten-fold or even a hundred-fold, as long as it's without the expectation of immediate and direct return? It blows me away how few people understand the power of this simple proposition. When you make someone else feel great, it can bring nothing but benefit to you, either directly or indirectly.

We live in selfish, competitive times, where scoring points *at* someone's expense seems to be more important than scoring points *with* them. We're so darn busy looking out for ourselves that we don't have any bandwidth left for anyone else. Big mistake. Big, fat, shortsighted, *dumb* mistake! Look, it costs next to nothing to make someone else feel like a million dollars, and the small amount it may cost will be one of the best investments you'll ever make.

I'm a busy man, but never too busy to take time to get hold of those high-demand tickets to help a friend impress his wife, send a bottle of champagne over to an acquaintance on his birthday, present a big box of chocolates to a neighbor who's going through a hard time, put a call in to try and secure a guy that job interview he so desperately needs, have a chat with someone's troubled son, or even chauffeur friends to their wedding in the Rolls. You can rely on me to come through, and you can rely on me to expect *nothing* in return. I know the return will come anyway, maybe indirectly, when all these folks spread the word about what a great guy I am!

And sometimes the benefit will be *immediately* tangible. A lead for a new client, an invitation to a great party, an endorsement, a new connection, doors opened and favors done. This is the *give-and-take of life*, and learning to cater with ease, style, and class will put you on a fast track to move past the wannabes into the ranks of the winners.

Why is it so difficult for most folks to grasp this simple truth? Why is it they think that when they put someone else center stage and demonstrate warmth and generosity, that it's a sign of weakness? Most people believe, it appears, that gifts should come with strings, that granting favors is all about gaining control, and that any kind of giving must be immediately reciprocated. And they believe that when you make someone feel good, somehow you've given away some kind of personal advantage—shown your hand, maybe, or let your guard down.

Like all of my other Streetwise Strategies, the best way to prove this one is to test it. From this moment on, I want you all to consider yourselves students of the catering business!

4   Take care of those who take care of you (doing things the Chicago way!)

This is really another aspect of catering, but with a "tactical" twist and a good chance of immediate return.

A little later, I'll be sharing the story of how I met my wife, but I can tell you now, that on our first date we met at a local bar in Chicago, which on a Friday night was standing room only. She got there early, and I arrived late (for a number of reasons). I barreled into the bar, more than a little anxious and out of breath, 'cause I was already smitten and had sprinted the last six blocks! While waiting for me, she'd navigated her way through the crowd, bought herself a drink, and been hit on by a couple of guys. Needless to say, by the time I blew in, she was less than impressed.

I knew I needed to make some moves fast. Well, fifty (discrete) bucks later, we were seated in VIP seats in an oasis of calm, fenced off by silk ropes from the seething mass of humanity crowding the bar. We ended up talking and laughing the night away. What can I say? The rest is history. Was fifty bucks expensive for a seat in a bar? Of course. Was it a small investment in the rest of my life? You bet. Best fifty bucks I ever spent! The point? Well, I certainly don't advocate anything that is unethical or illegal, but for heaven's sake, a few bucks, well-placed, isn't going to break the bank, and will open more doors than you believed possible.

And, money isn't the only valid *Chicago-way currency*. A smile, a word, a holiday gift, or a bouquet of flowers will make a difference, too. Hotel, car wash, parking garage, or bar, when you take care of those who take care of you, you'll stand out from the crowd, get that extra bit of attention, and be seen as a VIP. After all, it's only *fair trade.*

OPPORTUNITIES TO GET WHAT YOU WANT BY TIPPING

Are you only tipping your waiter? No wonder you're not receiving VIP treatment. Here are seven important people hustlers know to tip.

1 **Nightclub doorman.** Those people seated in the VIP section aren't all rich and famous. Most of them tipped their way past the velvet rope. Plan on spending $20 to $100 to get into the VIP section, depending upon the prestige of the club.

2 **Airport curbside baggage handler.** Your bags probably will still arrive if you don't tip, but you'll have better odds—particularly if you're running late—if you tip a few dollars per bag. If your bags are heavy or oversized, or if the handler helps you make your flight on time, tip more.

3 **Hotel maid.** It's customary to tip at least a couple of bucks per day for maid service, more if you've left a big mess. To avoid confusion, leave the bill on the pillow of your unmade bed. If you need extra towels or toiletries, they'll arrive faster and in greater supply than if you don't tip. Tipping also insures against theft, especially in the event you carelessly leave your valuables out in the open.

4 **Bartenders.** If you wonder why you stand for ages at the bar counter, waiting for service, or if your drinks always seem weak, you're probably not tipping enough. Tip at least 15–20 percent for each alcoholic drink served. Same goes for waitresses.

Savvy7

5 Hotel concierge. While hotels provide this service for free, a well-placed $10 or $20 will increase your odds of getting tickets to sold-out events or a reservation at the hottest restaurant in town.

6 Restaurant maitre d'. If you're hosting an important business dinner, or simply want to impress a date, tip the person in charge of seating guests. Make it clear from the beginning that you want a "power table" or romantic spot, and use a $20 bill to get your point across.

7 Teachers or daycare providers. While most teachers can't accept cash tips, a gift card to a bookstore, movie theater, or restaurant will go a long way in making up for any unruly behavior by your child. A tip won't buy better grades or even preferential treatment, but it will communicate that your child's welfare is a priority. Teachers and childcare providers tend to spend a little extra time with children if they know education is a parental priority.

5 Keep crackin' that whip!

Our ability to use words is one of our greatest assets.

When I was a kid, tangled in gang life, I learned to harness the incalculable power of words. Words were both armor and bullets, and far more effective than anything made of steel or stone. Most of us don't have a great *word strategy*. We talk to be heard, but not necessarily to say anything; we use words to gossip and whisper rather than to praise and motivate; we use them as defense rather than offense.

Think about it. Words define us. We use them to defuse conflict, forge bonds, vent our frustrations, express love and joy, sing our hearts out, pray, debate, discuss, and describe. *Words move lives forward, not battles.* Sometimes our words *soar* and sometimes they *sour*, but when you become a master of words, you can move mountains.

Of course, *silence* is a powerful weapon, too. It's the best negotiation tool in the world, in fact. Give it a go. Offer up some silence and see how the other guy rushes in to fill the void, and ends up giving away a lot more than he ever intended!

You've seen those movies where the detective, or the psychiatrist, lets silence hang out there as thick as fog, and the other guy ends up blurting out his confession. Well, you don't see it in a hundred movies for nothing. *Silence works.* A great place to try it is in your next meeting with friends or colleagues. Leave some empty space and see what flows into it.

I may be known as a man who's never at a loss for words, but you'll see me sitting back many a time and letting the conversation roll over me, as I quietly study the group dynamics and learn more about the other guy than he'll ever know about me. Give people the opportunity and they'll show you their whole game plan, but if you're clever with the poker face, they'll never know *yours*.

Though silence is a great tactical weapon, it's words that *ultimately win the game.* These days I try to learn a new word or two every week to expand my vocabulary. I'm involved with an organization—the "Ready to Learn Partnership"—that promotes early literacy through toys and multimedia interaction. It's designed to effectively teach kids to read and write, and to encourage their parents to teach through example and communicate like never before.

So, wherever I go, I continue to crack my whip motivatin', movin', and mobilizin'.

6 **Persevere: a winner never quits, and a quitter never wins**

I do not think there is any other quality so essential to success of any kind as the quality of perseverance. It overcomes almost everything, even nature.

John D. Rockefeller,
Industrialist and Philanthropist

This rule should really move to the top of my list, because there is nothing—nothing—*more vital* to success and *essential* to the good hustler than sheer, dogged determination and perseverance. All the mind jedi skills in the world, gallons of imagination, and bottomless optimism won't add up to jack if you give up too soon! Patience, discipline, and relentlessness will get you around, under, over, or through all the barriers you're inevitably going to crash into. Whatever happens, remember to *stay standin' on your square!*

> *Nothing in the world can take the place of persistence.*
> *Talent will not; nothing is more common than*
> *unsuccessful men with talent.*
> *Genius will not; unrewarded genius is almost a*
> *proverb. Education will not; the world is full of*
> *educated derelicts. Persistence and determination alone*
> *are omnipotent. The slogan, "press on," has solved,*
> *and always will solve, the problems of the human race.*
> **Calvin Coolidge,**
> **U.S. President**

7 Persist: every "no" only takes you one step closer to "yes"

To be doggedly persistent takes the right attitude. There's always some voice out there that's going to be tellin' you to give up, throw in the towel, and go home. It could be your family encouraging you to "settle," your workmates raising their eyebrows at your dreams, or a partner telling you to give yourself a break and lower your expectations, so you won't break your heart with disappointment.

They may all mean well, but the weight of their limited ambitions can't be allowed to drag you down. Now, here's the interesting thing: those guys are not the opponents you should be worrying about. In time, you'll learn to avoid them, ignore them, or just plain tune them out until they're nothing but white noise.

No, the loudest, most strident, most negative voice you'll hear, the one telling you that you just don't have what it takes, the one that's much harder to tune out, turn down, or turn off, is most likely to be your own!

In short, if you believe in yourself, then anything, is possible. If you don't have a certain bull-headedness, then you'll eventually come to a grinding halt.

> *If I had to select one quality, one personal*
> *characteristic that I regard as being most highly*
> *correlated with success, whatever the field,*
> *I would pick the trait of persistence. Determination.*
> *The will to endure to the end, to get knocked down*
> *seventy times and get up off the floor saying,*
> *"Here comes number seventy-one!"*
>
> **Richard M. DeVos,**
> **Co-founder of Amway**

Always remember that every "no" is just taking you one step closer to achieving your "yes." For every door that closes, hundreds more open. I encourage you to develop the mental tenacity of a fighter, a bruiser, a scrapper. Think *Rocky* 10! He'll still be goin' strong! Every "no" is a gauntlet thrown down, every bloody nose another reason to prove them wrong, and every crack on the jaw another reason to prove YOU right!

> *Fight one more round. When your arms are*
> *so tired that you can hardly lift your hands*
> *to come on guard, fight one more round.*
> *When your nose is bleeding and your eyes are black*
> *and you are so tired that you wish*
> *your opponent would crack you one on the jaw*
> *and put you to sleep, fight one more round—*
> *remembering that the man who always fights*
> *one more round is never whipped.*
>
> **James Corbett,**
> **Heavyweight Boxing Champion (Gentleman Jim)**

8 Remember a small fish beats an empty dish

*Don't be afraid to give your best to what seemingly are
small jobs. Every time you conquer one it makes you
that much stronger. If you do the little jobs well,
the big ones will tend to take care of themselves.*

**Dale Carnegie,
Lecturer and Writer on Self-Improvement**

There are many great men, who started off doing menial jobs, and yet worked themselves up to positions of unimaginable power and wealth. The true *good hustler* never shies away from small tasks because he knows they are only steppingstones to much greater things.

REAL TALK
Veronica was at her wit's end when she came to me. Her only child, Robert, was headed down a dangerous path. He'd been messin' with some real gangstas, and she suspected he was dealing drugs. She'd tried talking to him, but he didn't want to hear it. Her husband, Robert's stepdad, owned ten fast food franchises and tried to help out by offering Robert a job as a management trainee. Robert balked at the offer—it was beneath him!

Man, I can't tell you how many times I've heard stories like this. Not only about the gangs and the drugs, but how people expect to catapult straight to the top, bypassing all the rungs of the ladder. Corporate or street, these power climbers share a common sense of entitlement, believing that they deserve money, power, and status from the get-go.

Well, you know I gave Rob a straight-shootin', no-sugar-coatin' talkin' to the day we met. I put it to him real—the road he was on had two destinations: the

REAL TALK

penitentiary or the morgue. If he was lucky enough to get locked up, he'd need even more luck to survive the experience. And if he thought his stepdad's job offer was insulting, he should try a prison job, working in the kitchen or the laundry room, or maybe even sewing the pockets on the jeans his friends would be wearing on the outside. Oh, he'd get paid all right—maybe $15 or $16 a month!

Now tell me, Rob, I asked, how much lower can you get than that? Here he was, a kid with a great opportunity, a real hook-up, and he was throwing it away without a second thought.

Go to work for your stepdad, I told him, and give it your very best, every minute of every day. Soon you'll be running the joint, and then the other nine joints, and then twenty! Before you know it, I continued, you'll be a wealthy entrepreneur, the richest guy in town, and maybe even make the cover of *Fortune* magazine! Now, I don't know where Rob ended up, but let's hope it was behind the counter, not behind bars.

9 **Fail to prepare, prepare to fail . . .**

Life is not fair. The moment you take your eye off the game, it'll throw you a curve ball fast enough to knock your teeth out. There are times when I screw up and get so mad at myself I can hardly catch my breath. You see, I know better than to let anything take me unaware, sneak up from behind, and find me napping. Heck, I'm a street guy, indoctrinated to "expect the worst" so as to deflect it before it actually occurs. When I walk down the street, I'm scanning the crowd. When I go into a restaurant, I sit facing the door so I can see who comes and goes. When I'm out and about at night, it's with acute awareness of everything going on around me. And you won't see me hangin' in the kind of places where trouble is just waiting to happen, or putting myself in harm's way. No way. Not this guy.

Now my street lessons have all been learned the hard way through trial and error, screw-ups, and carelessness, and may not seem at all relevant to you as you look out the window of your nice suburban house or downtown office. But the reality is, the streets are a microcosm of the world we all share, magnified a thousand-fold. If you are prepared to take the time to understand the dynamics of the streets, then you will already have your finger on the pulse points of everywhere else that matters, from corporate America to rural Ohio to Wisteria Lane.

After all, human dynamics are universal.

The guy walking toward you may not have a knife in his pocket, but that won't stop him from stickin' one in your back. Your boss may be an Ivy League graduate, but that doesn't mean he's not a bully. And the guy on the treadmill next to you may drive a BMW, but that won't stop him from stealin' your iPod the moment your back is turned! You may have been deeply in love with your ex for twenty years, but that won't get in the way of him, or her, taking you to the cleaners the moment the divorce papers are filed.

I can hear you now: "Do you always look for the bad in people, Burrel? That's a terrible way to live." Heck, no, I don't always look for the bad. The opposite in fact. I see the good in the majority of folks; but, I'm a realist, too. We've already talked about how just about everyone is hustling through life, trying to get an edge. Unfortunately, some of those folks are simply more predatory than others.

I'll say it again. *To hustle is to be human.* As long as you stay alert, prepared, and on your toes, you'll retain the advantage. Look, I'm a guy who makes a mistake one time and one time only—and, man, do I hate it when I do! Because I know better. I know you've gotta be prepared *all* the time—not *some* of the time. After all, fail to prepare and you'd better be prepared to fail.

The more you sweat in practice,
the less you bleed in battle.

Unknown

10 Turn the lesson into a blessin' and move on

As my dad used to say: "Every day is either a lesson or a blessin'." Sometimes it's hard to find either. Bad times, it seems, like company and travel in packs. Bad days usually come in clusters, too, and before you know it, they've shape-shifted into a *bad week*. Now, if enough bad weeks stack up, you begin to expect them all to be bad—and, of course, they will be, because we usually get what we expect. Now you've got a *bad life*.

Truth is most bad days are made up of a collection of irritating, inconvenient, and uncomfortable *small stuff*. On its own, none of these events are enough to derail you, but added together, they begin to feel like a CIA conspiracy.

You wake up and stub your toe getting out of bed. You limp into the shower, only to find that there's no hot water left. Still shivering from that chilling experience, you stub your toe again, on the way to the sink, only to discover the toothpaste tube is empty. You manage to get dressed, grab breakfast, and get out the door only about ten minutes later than usual. You might make it to work before the meeting starts.

And then, the car won't start.

Bet you've had your share of days like that.

The only way to *neutralize* bad days is to refuse to allow the small stuff—each individual irritation—to knock you down a notch. Instead, turn them into pluses. Remember what Grandma always said? *"If it's not a blessin', it's a lesson!"*

Trouble is only opportunity in work clothes.

Henry Kaiser,
Industrialist

Let me give you an example. I had one of those days recently, when it seemed like every way I turned, I was being ambushed by bad-luck ninjas. I mean, the day was just one challenge after another. I was coming down with a cold to begin with (forgot to wear a hat in wintry NYC), then the bank messed up some financial transfers, which got me into hot water and wasted my morning, then I received bad news about a friend, then a trip I'd been looking forward to was cancelled, then—the grand finale—when I was working out at the gym, I got sidetracked helping out a guy with some weights, and some *you-know-what* swiped my precious iPod and Bose headset from my treadmill! The loss was greater than you might think, because I'd stored hours of music, speeches, and motivational material on that iPod.

I was pretty miffed, I can tell you. Truth is, I was sizzlin'. I think I could have done with a bit of life coaching myself that day! For a moment, I forgot my own mantra of turning lemons into lemonade—but only for a moment. After a quick rant, I took a deep breath, regained perspective, and looked for the lesson in the experience. You can take it from me, I won't ever again make the mistake of being lulled into a false sense of security by exclusive surroundings. My gym is one of those upscale celebrity gyms, where I take my high-profile clients. And since I go every day myself, the luxury amenities are worth the price. But fact is, I let the classiness of the place knock me off my square.

Then, of course, there's the blessin' to consider: maybe I learned this lesson so I'd be smarter in the future, and avoid losing something even more precious to me. Maybe, without this lesson, I might have lost some of my precious (emotionally as well as dollar-wise!) jewelry, or my phone with all my contacts . . . Fact is, bad days happen if you let them get you down. Nip them in the bud, take the lesson, break the pattern, and move on.

11 Don't talk about it; be about it!

Corporate America's going to talk itself to death! I swear. I've sat through more meetings, committees, panels, and "feedback" sessions in the last five years than during the thirty-five that preceded them. Mind you L.A's not much better. Meet and greet, meet and eat, or just plain meet. Now, as y'all know, I love words, but at some point, they have to be matched by actions. Stop sittin', stop stewin', and stop stallin'! Time to take action. Bite-size or king-size, action beats hot air any day.

And here's another thing. I'm an advocate of "fakin' it 'till you make it." That means you have to shine on the outside while you polish up on the inside. A quick word of warning though: don't get sucked into believing the "fake" you. After all, if you spend all your time fakin', there'll be no time left for makin'!

In short: keep it real . . .

12 Never, ever, take a penitentiary chance

"A penitentiary chance, is he crazy?" I can just hear you saying. "He's the ex-gangster, not me. Of course, I'm not going to do anything that would put me in the pen! A speeding ticket, sure, but jail? Not a chance!"

Don't panic and don't take me too literally, because when I talk about taking *penitentiary chances* that's just my shorthand for "don't squander everything you've worked so hard to achieve by taking stupid risks." True, successful people take risks all the time. The key is to figure out if it is a *smart risk* or a dumb one.

> *Why not go out on a limb?*
> *Isn't that where the fruit is?*
>
> **Frank Scully,**
> **Author**

A *dumb risk* is no different than a gamble. The only person who wins is the house. Some folks seem to think that gambling and risk taking is the same thing. To me, that's a bit like saying, "If you throw your money into a hole in the ground, you may grow gold."

Gambling is a loser's game. Sorry, but that's the reality. You may win nine hands, but you'll lose the tenth. You may come out ahead this year, but you won't next. You may win big today, but you will lose bigger tomorrow.

I understand risk is part of life. You won't progress unless you take some chances and make some mistakes along the way. But when the price of the risk is too high, and threatens life, liberty, family, or friends—don't be tempted to take it.

When the potential prize seems to good to be true, it probably *is*.

Savvy 7

GET OUT THERE NOW!

The key to success is being out and about, and open to new opportunities. If you've been off the radar for awhile, try joining a social network, which is nothing more than a group of people with similar professions or interests. Don't limit yourself to subjects you're already comfortable with; instead, join a group that participates in an activity you aspire to. The following are some popular choices:

1 Toastmasters teaches members to be successful businesspeople. Local Toastmaster clubs of twenty to thirty people meet once a week and focus on topics such as leadership, public speaking, and management skills. Visit www.toastmaster.com.

2 Do you enjoy reading? Book clubs are more popular than ever. If you can't find one on your own, search online at www.readerscircle.org.

3 Rotary clubs tackle projects that give back to the community. Not only will you feel good about serving the community, you'll make great contacts, because many Rotarians are successful business leaders. Visit www.rotary.org.

Savvy7

4 Alumni organizations provide excellent opportunities to meet new people. Universities with successful sports programs often have viewing parties across the country in which local alumni get together to watch football or basketball games. Visit your university's Web site for more information.

5 Professional organizations are meant to encourage professional networking, but often result in social opportunities. If you're normally shy in new social situations, a professional organization will provide a built-in conversational topic you can use to break the ice.

6 Hook up with old classmates through www.friendsreunited.com.

7 Online social networks are gaining in popularity and provide many social networking opportunities. MySpace isn't just for teenagers; in fact, you'll find me there!

YA GOTTA DO IT

HUSTLE WITH HEART

Having a hard time getting started networking? It's easy to get excited about meeting new people when you have a common bond with them, like a favorite hobby or interest. And it sure solves the problem of finding something to talk about. Pick something you like to do, whether it's fantasy football or walking dogs at the animal shelter, and get involved! You can join a local group that meets in person, or you can join the many online virtual communities. Do it today and start hustling—with heart!

11

STREETWISE STRATEGY #3: PAY YOURSELF FIRST EVERY DAY

It's tough to do, but you've got to work at living, you know? Most people work at dying, but anybody can die; the easiest thing on this earth is to die. But to live takes guts; it takes energy, vitality; it takes thought. . . . We have so many negative influences out there that are pulling us down. . . . You've got to be strong to overcome these adversities . . . that's why I never stop."

Jack La Lanne
"The Godfather of Fitness"

We all spend a lot of time paying. We pay the bills. We pay the price. We pay visits, and we pay debts. We pay dues, and we payback. But how often do we pay ourselves?

Not often enough.

Most of us are our own toughest taskmasters. We drive ourselves hard and generally don't give time off for good behavior—or give ourselves much of a paycheck either, for that matter. I've discovered that few people really understand what "paying yourself first" actually means.

You might choose to reward yourself for a job well done, saying to yourself: "I've been working like a dog. I've had my head down and feel like I've been run over by a steamroller. It's time for a reward: a trip to the spa, a day off work, or a day at the beach." Any, or all, of these are good healthy things to do, but frankly none of these "time-outs" is enough. Besides, let's keep it real. It's much more likely that you'll fall back on the *same old same old:* a big, greasy dinner that leaves you bloated, or a happy hour that turns into an unhappy morning!

Real personal reward comes in a form you might least expect. Exercise. Yup, that painful, sweaty hard labor called *exercise* is the very best *personal paycheck* you will ever give yourself!

REAL TALK

David's Story

"It's like a light went on. I'd been struggling for a long time. I had money worries, women worries, work worries, and couldn't seem to get my head up. It started with Burrel getting me to work out. He explained to me that a strong mind and body went together. I began running. I wasn't overweight, though I must admit I did think I was fitter than I was.

"When I started running, it was hard, and—I'll keep it real—I complained a lot. I wasn't happy. I couldn't see how this was going to change anything. This was adding more stress, not making things easier, I thought. Then something sort of clicked. I got hooked on it. I could see the changes to my body, felt strong and energized, but, even more important, felt my confidence going through the roof.

"I used the running time for thinking, clearing my mind, and just taking stock of things. Man, I can't even begin to tell you how my life has changed in the eighteen months since I started working with Burrel. All my worries seemed to get smaller and the opportunities bigger. Things were just much clearer to me. And, well, less dramatic. I wasn't as emotional. I was focused. I started walking differently, dressing differently, and, heck, dreaming differently!

"I felt totally in control. First time in a long time. Now that's the best feeling in the world."

Transformation is driven from the inside-out, but is accelerated from the outside-in. What do I mean? Well, while it's true we have to break down the mental *success barriers* inside our heads, it's easier to build mental muscle when you simultaneously build physical fitness too, through exercise and discipline. This is the simple secret to *turbo-charging your total transformation.* Ask anyone—I preach exercise like it was a religion.

Don't ever doubt that a strong body is crucial to cultivating a strong mind. This doesn't mean you gotta run marathons, do two hundred push-ups a day, climb mountains, or grow prison-yard biceps. It does mean, though, that you show yourself the greatest respect of all, by taking pride in, and care of, your body.

As you watch your body strengthen, tone, and evolve, your whole attitude to life evolves as well. Each time you exercise, it's like giving yourself a reward, a personal paycheck. Instead of working for "the man," simply to pay the bills, you're doing this for you, for your family, for life.

Savvy7

EXERCISE BENEFITS

The world-renowned Mayo Clinic released this list of seven exercise benefits[1]:

1 Strengthens your heart and lungs.

2 Keeps bones and muscles strong.

3 Helps you achieve and maintain healthy body weight.

4 Prevents and manages diabetes.

5 Fights depression and helps manage stress.

6 Reduces risk of cancer.

7 Improves sleep.

So how to get started? If you're like 99.9 percent of the rest of the population, you've been wrestling with the exercise bogeyman for quite some time, so now it's time to shift your mind all the way around.

- **STOP imagining the effort and START visualizing the fresh, energized YOU.** Imagine that every step taken, every mile run, every weight lifted adds a day to your life and a point to your IQ, while taking a millimeter from your waistline and a load off your mind!

- **STOP focusing on the punishment and START focusing on the payback.** Every drop of sweat, every heartbeat, every strain of a muscle lifts you that little bit closer to becoming the fit, strong, healthy person you always dreamed of being—and one step closer to slipping into that svelte suit you haven't bought yet (but will)!

1. Mayo Foundation for Medical Education and Research (MFMER), Mayo Clinic Staff, published July 26, 2005, on www.mayoclinic.com.

- **STOP thinking of exercise as a pain and START thinking of it as a privilege.** Imagine for a moment if you were forbidden to move. That some person told you, you must sit at your desk and not budge for a month. Worse yet, imagine you're locked in a tiny cell, eighteen hours a day, with no fresh air, no sunlight, and no room to move. For fifty years.

Now think about striding out into the sunshine, strong and free, running along the beach breathing in the tangy, salty air, skiing down a crisp white slope, the wind in your face and the snow swooshing up in a fine white mist all around you, or enjoying the simple pleasure of strolling around the yard, walking down the street, or running toward a loved one at the airport.

So why the heck do we hate exercise so much?

Remember when you were a kid and you couldn't sit still? You were always on the go, always into mischief. Remember how you loved running around, playing games, and wrestling with your brother on the grass? Playing tag, and hide and seek with the other kids?

How much movin' for fun do you do today?

Here's the thing. When we stop exercising, we get smaller. Yes, we *shrink*. No, I don't mean you'll lose inches—and unless you waste away, you certainly won't lose pounds—but you still shrink. You curl up around yourself, hunch over your desk and your worries, and diminish. So you may not lose inches, but you'll lose confidence. You may not lose pounds, but you'll lose perspective. Guaranteed.

You see, *exercise is a privilege, not a pain.*

We crave freedom, we're programmed for movement, and we loathe forced stillness. There are people who have lost their limbs and natural mobility, but will move heaven and earth to find ways to keep moving around in the world, on wheels or prosthetics. They undergo brutal physical therapy to mobilize their bodies. They run marathons, ski mountains, and swim oceans. Look at the Paralympics for a thousand examples of determination, courage, and supreme physical endeavor.

Now take a hard look at yourself. Why are so many of us, who are fit, strong, and sound, just vegetating shamefully? If vegetating were our natural state, we'd have all been born green.

The intent of this thought-stream isn't to beat up on you for not working out—a carrot generally works way better than a stick—but it is designed to suggest that you *flip the script* when you think about exercise. Take all your preconceptions and turn them on their head. Think of how you would feel if you couldn't exercise—if you were in poor health, trapped, broken, or imprisoned. Now think about that toned, fit, strong person you're gonna be in only a few short months, because you've decided to *pay yourself first every day with exercise,* and because you're privileged enough to be able to make that choice.

I started running about three years ago. I run around twenty-five miles a week now, but it took me a while to get there. I started off slowly, just some power walking, and gradually built up to a few miles a day. Soon I added a bit of jogging, and now, I speed along like a greyhound* with a smile on my face all the way.

Is it easy? Never. Some days the thought of the treadmill makes me cringe, but I've learned to not listen to that warm and drowsy little inner voice telling me to stay in bed another hour instead. No, I quickly learned that inner voice was my own internal *Player Hater,* and whenever it got too loud, I realized it wouldn't even exist if I didn't allow it to.

> *I'm a big advocate of recreational sports.*
> *If I can get out there, even if it's a hike or*
> *something like that, just to break up the monotony*
> *of going to the gym . . . I really like that.*
> **Jessica Biel,**
> **Actor**

---

* Okay, a very slow greyhound!

154

TIPS TO STICK WITH AN EXERCISE PROGRAM

If exercise programs were easy, everybody would be fit. Try these seven tips to help pay yourself back—every day.

1 Focus on developing a good exercise habit first, then try to lose weight. Would you try to fly across the country by hopping into an airplane cockpit without first learning how to pilot a plane? Of course not! To lose weight and get fit, you first need to learn how to integrate exercise into your daily routine. Skip this important step, and you'll probably fail.

2 Keep an exercise log. A written record will create accountability, and you'll be able to look back upon your accomplishments when you need motivation. If you're a runner, keep track of how many miles you run each day, week, month, and year. You'll have plenty to be proud of.

3 It's an oldie but a goodie—display an item of clothing you were able to wear at your ideal weight, or one you want to wear some day. When you see it, visualize how you used to be disciplined or how you want to be.

4 Listen to your body. If you haven't exercised in awhile, you will experience some discomfort. In the beginning, do your best to discern between conditioning pain and injury pain.

5 Stretch before and after your workout. Tightened and short muscles can pull on your spine and joints, causing injuries even after you've left the gym. Don't "cheat" by stretching with incorrect posture or alignment. Rounding your back to touch your toes doesn't provide nearly as many benefits as properly stretching your quadriceps with a flat back.

Savvy7

6 Invest in good equipment. Don't go out running or walking in cheap shoes. Spend the money to provide proper support and function for any equipment you need.

7 Treat your workout time like a business appointment. Remember, you're learning to pay yourself first. That means meeting the obligations you've set for yourself, every time.

YOU ARE WHAT YOU EAT

I'm no nutritionist, so I won't advise you on what might be the best diet for you, but I can tell you what works for me. All the diet plans and fads become so overwhelming that it's often hard to see your way through all the confusing advice that, often as not, contradicts itself. I'd like to share with you some of the simple discoveries I've made, and the diet and lifestyle I've chosen to adopt (which helps me feel younger today than I did ten years ago!)

For the most part, I follow a basic, common-sense healthy diet: lots of fresh fruits and vegetables, lean proteins, and low-glycemic carbs. I only have alcohol on special occasions, and rarely touch fast food or overprocessed vending machine junk. Every morning I'm at home, I make myself a smoothie, so I'm going to share my Savvy 7 favorite smoothie recipes. I'm also going to share a list of my Savvy 7 favorite healthy foods.

Savvy7

MY FAVORITE SMOOTHIES

A few general tips: You can use frozen or fresh fruit, but if you use fresh, add a few ice cubes to the mix to cool and thicken.

I personally prefer soy or almond milk to dairy product, and they are generally pretty interchangeable, but don't forget flavored milks will be sweet.

Finally, don't be afraid to experiment with healthy "additives." Add wheat germ, spirulina powder, ground-up flaxseed, or protein powders as directed on their packaging—some flavors will work, some won't, but soon you'll have designed your own custom mix!

Savvy7

1 The Hustle-Berry

½ cup fresh or frozen assorted berries such as raspberries, blackberries, and strawberries
1 cup orange juice
3 tablespoons vanilla low-fat yogurt
Small sprig of fresh mint (optional)

Tip: A spoonful of Royal Jelly will add a little more hustle to your berry!

2 Jedi Juice

1 cup apple juice
1 tablespoon honey
1 cup frozen or fresh organic strawberries
1 cup strawberry frozen yogurt

Tip: Ginkgo biloba is said to give a boost to blood circulation and memory—great for all you Mind Jedis out there! Be sure to follow brand label recommendations on dosage.

3 Protein Paycheck

1 banana, peeled and "chunked"
½ cup of yogurt
1 cup nonfat or soy milk
1 tablespoon protein powder (or recommended amount)

Tip: For an extra protein boost, add a powdered egg protein.

4 The Green Giant

> 4–5 ripe pears
> 4–5 leaves of kale
> ½ bunch of mint
> A sprig of parsley
> Water

Tip: Green smoothies are nutritious. Experiment with celery, romaine lettuce, parsley, kale, and spinach. Aim for around 55–60 percent ripe organic fruit topped with organic green vegetables.

5 Mango Magnetism

> 2 ripe peaches
> 1 mango
> ½ lemon
> 1 handful white seedless grapes OR 1 cup white grape juice

Tip: This smoothie is packed with vitamins, good for the immune system, and not too bad for healthy skin either.

6 Strawberry Success

> 2 cups frozen strawberries
> 3 cups lemonade
> ½ cup fruit sorbet
> 1 tablespoon protein powder

Tip: Mango, orange, lemon, or raspberry sorbet all work well, but be sure to add only in the final stages of blending.

Savvy**7**

7 Fair Play Frappuccino

1 (small) cup of coffee, chilled
1 banana cut into chunks
½ cup soy milk

Tip: For a sweet tooth, use vanilla or chocolate soy milk.

Savvy**7**

MY SAVVY 7 SUPER-FOODS

1 MonaVie juice. This fruit extract supplement gives me energy and makes me feel great! MonaVie is a blended juice that includes the Brazilian acai berry—a powerful antioxidant and nutrient. If MonaVie is a little rich for you, the Goji juice is also a great buy.

2 Fruit and protein smoothies made with soy milk and a sprinkle of protein powder or bee pollen.

3 Steamed endamame soy beans (sprinkled lightly with sea salt) and other great green veggies.

4 Almonds and walnuts.

5 Poached and grilled fish, and, of course, sashimi and sushi.

6 Lots and lots of cool, clear water.

7 The right blend of vitamins and supplements. Even though my diet includes most of my daily allowances, I like to add a boost.

Tom's Story (Part 2)

Let's get back to Tom. Remember him, Mr. Popeye's Chicken 2003? He was boxed in by his own negative attitude, a dead-end career, and life. Well, at least he was when I met him.

First on the to-do list was some serious reprogramming. We spent the majority of our time straight-talkin' and identifying the behaviors that put Tom in his predicament in the first place.

We didn't really start making progress until we got him into the gym. And at first, it was a real struggle. He'd bitch and moan, and let me tell you, getting Tom to move was like putting your shoulder against a Hummer and trying to push it backwards, uphill, with the brakes on.

But move, he finally did. More often, faster, and eventually on his own! After about eight months, Tom had lost more than forty pounds of fat and put on about twenty pounds of solid muscle. He was stronger, fitter, and healthier than he'd been even back when he was a star.

And not only that, but his confidence, optimism, and energy levels shot through the roof. He could now look back on his old situation with a new perspective. He finally realized he'd built his own prison, one chicken leg at a time, and had locked his mind and body behind closed doors.

Tom has since moved and started a new life and career in Phoenix, where he is now a successful real estate agent. Like that saying from Shakespeare,

Tom realized the whole world is a stage, and it's best to take an active role in that production called "life." Thanks to Tom's attitude adjustment, he didn't run from the entertainment biz, he ran toward a new and exciting life. Now that's going somewhere!

REWARD YOURSELF WITH LOVE

I'm going to share another of the "worst kept secrets" in the world. Success will be forever elusive, and you a weaker person—much, much weaker—if you can't count people who care for you deeply among your inner circle of friends, family, and colleagues.

Now to some this may seem counterintuitive. "If I fly solo," they say, "and avoid emotional attachments or emotional responsibility for anyone else, it'll give me an edge." They believe that without distractions, they can focus on channeling all their mind power toward wealth creation, unhindered by the neediness of others.

Wrong. *Very wrong!*

Great relationships are essential for a number of reasons. They provide the solid foundation on which everything else is built. If your personal life is in constant turmoil, or worse, nonexistent, then you've no real "center of gravity" to keep you grounded. They provide sustenance and support. They help you to be less selfish and more generous and considerate. And, of course, they help provide a check and balance between work and personal life.

For many people, a great relationship is not the key to success; it is the very *definition of success.*

I'm always amazed at the number of guys, led by their testosterone, who are always chasing the next cheap thrill, often at the expense of the woman who has been by their side for years. Look, I'm not a holier-than-thou kind of guy. Face it, with my history that's never gonna happen. No, this isn't about *judging.* It's just plain common sense. Think of a great relationship as a kind of emotional balance sheet, and the bottom line is: *love pays.*

There's nothing more powerful than having a partner in your life who's behind you, or even in front of you, every step of the way. They're hard to find, though, so why after investing years in figuring each other out, sharing experiences, and building the kind of trust that money can't buy, *why* would you ever want to trade it all for the fleeting satisfaction of a fling or two?

It's true, I've had a few relationships that didn't last, but believe me, when I'm in it, I'm in it! The only competition any woman in my life ever faced was my love of the *game* and my addiction to the *deal.*

I mean how can I NOT vote for the person who votes for me?

Six secrets for "flowing" relationships

1 **Stop competing with each other:** Good relationships are all about being on the same side. What's the purpose in scoring all those points? Sure you may cross the finish line first today, and maybe tomorrow as well. But you'll be all alone when you do, and if you carry on this way, eventually you may not have anyone left in your life to compete with! So stop competing. Start concentrating on crossing that finish line as part of a winning team.

2 **Listen, communicate, and hear:** One of my favorite parts of my great marriage is to sit and chat with my wife. We talk about big stuff and small stuff, share plans and pains, and each of us respects what the other is saying. We never use silence as a weapon, and we never go to bed mad. Master the simple art of real conversation, and your relationship is halfway home.

3 **Understand a relationship is not about "ownership":** This is probably the most common personal problem I come across in my life-coaching capacity. Possessiveness and jealousy are two of the most destructive of all human forces. Few relationships will survive the poison of this twin-horned devil. Let it go!

4 **Pay yourself first every day:** We've talked a lot about the fact that the most important relationship of all is the one you have with yourself, and that requires that you take care of your body, mind, and spirit every single day. It's called *self-respect.* I can guarantee that if you don't care for yourself, then few others have any incentive to do so either. Why should they respect you if you don't? Take care of yourself first each

day, so you can be strong enough to look out for the people *you* care about.

5 **Put the romance back:** You simply can't beat it. A romantic gesture says: "At this moment, I am thinking 100 percent of you and your needs, and I want to do everything I can to please you." It also says much about your own confidence and style. You'd be amazed how many people are motivated to make romantic gestures because of the praise they'll receive, not the pleasure they'll give. That isn't romance; it's selfishness. Learn to discern. Become a *master of romance*. It'll spice up your life.

6 **Learn how to bend, but never so far that you snap:** Relationships are all about *give and take*. It's okay to bend with the wind sometimes. That's the nature of the dance. But it's not okay to bow over so far, so often, and so low, that you get worn down, weaken, and snap. Learn how much to give, how much to take, and when to walk away.

Just one last word on this subject: Being in a relationship is a bit like being on a see-saw. No matter how great it would be to be on the same level all the time, you and your partner are seldom going to find yourselves equally balanced. So one minute you're up, the next you're down.

Sometimes, it seems as though you're the one who's always down and your partner up. If that happens, you might begin to look at your partner with resentment—as though somehow it's his or her fault that you're firmly stuck in the mud while he or she is flying high.

But whose fault is it really? Think about it. Isn't it the role of the person sitting on the lower part of the see-saw, the one who's closest to the ground, to use his force to propel himself back up to the high point again? So rather than spend your time feeling jealous and bitter, you might want to be working on strengthening those leg muscles.

*I learned about the strength you can get
from a close family life.
I learned to keep going, even in bad times.
I learned not to despair, even
when my world was falling apart.
I learned that there are no free lunches.
And I learned the value of hard work.*

**Lee Iacocca,
Automotive Industry Leader**

YA GOTTA DO IT

PAY YOURSELF FIRST EVERY DAY

Not a gym person? You don't have to do bicep curls or run five miles to enjoy the benefits of exercise. Try putting on some music or finding a cable station that plays videos from when you were in high school. Then, dance around the room to your heart's content—and if you have small children or a spouse who's game, get them to dance with you! Nothing will get your heart pumping, the sweat flowing, and your spirits lifted faster than dancing like when you were a shorty.

12

STREETWISE STRATEGY #4: BECOME A SUCCESS MAGNET

*Man, this guy is something else!
He has an amazingly positive energy
that just never turns off. He's larger
than life. He's unique and I love him.
If you get the chance to bring him
into your life—do.*

Corey Maggette,
Professional Basketball Player

People ask me every day: "How come you're always so cheerful, Burrel? How on Earth do you manage to keep smiling every day?"

We all have days when it's tougher to smile than others, and I, for one, blend a good bit of cold-eyed pragmatism into my view of the world (hey, I'm an optimist, not a sucker), but I know, too, that *positive* is the only way to go. We'll explore this area in more depth shortly, but the fact is, *I LOVE life* and appreciate every moment that I get to inhale in a little more of it.

Okay. So maybe you're completely *over* all this positive thinking stuff. Heard it all before, read the book, bought the T-shirt. "Too late for positive, dude," I hear you say. "A good chunk has already been taken out of my hide. Fact is, life has gnawed on me like a ham bone. I don't have an ounce of optimism left."

You count up a few of the bad things that have happened to you, compare yourself to a few of the "luckier guys," point a blame finger or two, and there you are, knee-deep in a mess of disappointment and self-pity. Truth is, cynicism is easier than optimism, defeatism easier than excitement, wallowing easier than shining. Optimism, on the other hand, takes energy, faith, determination, and, yes, work.

> *A cynic is a man who knows the price of everything but the value of nothing.*
>
> **Oscar Wilde,**
> **Playwright and Poet**

While cynicism is an easy fallback, it's also a deadly trap, because like any other behavior, if you practice it often enough, it becomes a habit—*a bad habit.* There's no place for defeatism, negativity, or blame-gaming in a successful life. We each make our own success, and if you don't like the hand you've been dealt, you best pick yourself up, brush yourself off, pull your chair up to the table, and deal yourself a few new cards!

HOW TO BECOME POSITIVELY MAGNETIC!

My first practical lesson on *magnetism* came about in my gangster days when Wenny—my childhood best friend—and I ran a few very profitable gambling dens on Chicago's West Side. We were making a ton of money on dice and card games. Today, as you know, I don't gamble. I don't support gambling, and I actually spend quite a bit of time explaining to other folks why gambling is a fool's game. But, back in the day, I was a serious gambler. On one wild, regrettable, unforgettable occasion I lost millions of bucks in a single wager!

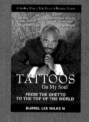

We knew a guy who manufactured very clever dice tables. Both table and dice were magnetized. Don't ask me to explain the science, but a magnetic field either attracts or repels another based on the positive or negative force of each. With the press of a button the force of the table could be adjusted. In short, we could *gimmick* the die to fall whichever way the house needed them to.

Controls were cleverly integrated into a silver belt buckle. I became highly adept at pressing the right buttons, using only sense of touch. I usually had custody of the belt while Wiz moved the game along. Being careful not to overplay our hand, we'd rotate the renegade tabletop between locations but if through-traffic was good, the games lively, and the takings healthy, we'd put it to bed for the night. No point in spoiling a good thing.—From *Tattoos on My Soul*

Over the years, however, I learned to harness the power of magnetism in much more *responsible* way. You see, if you try to force two magnets together, the positive force of each will repel them away from each other. You can actually feel the force of one pushing the other away. Now, strangely enough, with people—completely in defiance of the laws of physics—the exact opposite is true!

When it comes to humans, *positive force attracts more positive force.*

● Positive mental images attract positive results.

● Positive attitudes attract positive reactions.

● Positive appearances attract positive perceptions.

● Positive people expect good things to happen to them, and good things do, indeed, happen.

I've always been a positive guy. Gregarious, extroverted, expressive, and, yes, loud! (Although, oddly enough, I spent the first eighteen months of my life silent, sitting quietly on the floor, amidst the Wilks' family chaos, not cryin' or crawlin'. Then, one day, I decided to join the party, and I haven't stopped since.)

People enjoy being around positive energy. It's energizing to bask in its warmth, and recharge yourself with its high-voltage electricity. Want to add more juice to your positive "charge"? It's simple—just turn on the "happy channel."

TURN ON THE HAPPY CHANNEL

*Burrel is always smiling. Not a put-on, plastic kind
of smile, but the kind of high-voltage beam that
illuminates rooms and warms Chicago winters.*

Larry B. (friend)

In the book *Being Peace*[1], a Buddhist monk named Thich Nhat Hanh says, "You know the effect of a smile. A smile can relax hundreds of muscles in your face, and relax your nervous system. A smile makes you master of yourself. When you smile, you realize the wonder of the smile."

My wife shared Hanh's work with me because she was intrigued at the consistency between some of my Streetwise Strategies and Hanh's more spiritual teachings on the subject of positivism, happiness, and peace.

I couldn't agree more with Hanh. Smiling as therapy for body and soul is a great concept, and as essential to your daily workout routine as cardio or weights are. I mean, physical exercise may work your gluts, biceps, or lungs, and strengthen your mind and spirit, too; but, smiling is the best workout I know, not only for your face, but for your heart and soul, too. For years, I've promoted turning on the happy channel.

---

1. *Being Peace,* Thich Nhat Hanh, Parallax Press, 1996.

A human being is like a television set with millions
of channels . . . If we turn sorrow on, we are sorrow.
If we turn a smile on, we really are the smile.
We cannot let just one channel dominate us.
We have the seed of everything in us, and
we have to seize the situation in our hand,
to recover our own sovereignty.
Thich Nhat Hanh,
Author and Peace Activist

Yes, when you smile, the whole world smiles with you. It may be corny and it may be clichéd, but clichés exist for a reason—they're generally TRUE! Still don't believe in the force of a smile? Then I *dare* you to try it out. Tomorrow. As you go about your daily business, make a conscious effort to make eye contact, smile at, and have a word with your neighbor, the postman, the guy you see on the train every day, the doorman, the receptionist, the FedEx man—whomever!

Now don't roll your eyes at me. I'm serious. I meet more people, have more fascinating conversations, and make more productive contacts by simply smiling and taking a moment to wish someone a great day.

- I met my wife when I smiled at her as she drove past me on the freeway (yes, really!).

- I met an influential business contact when we stopped to compare watches.

- I met one of my agents at a gas station. We'd both stopped at the pumps to fill up; I saw her Chicago plates and introduced myself.

- I met one of my closest friends today at a social event more than twenty years ago, when I broke the ice and started chatting with him.

- I met Bill, a guy who has become a regular client, when we sat next to each other on the plane from L.A. to New York.

BURREL'S SEVEN STREETWISE STRATEGIES

A good laugh is sunshine in a house.

**William Makepeace Thackeray,
Novelist**

You'll probably—no, make that definitely—be rebuffed by a few of the folks you approach, but don't take it personally. Some people, wrapped up in their own thoughts and worries, are too taken aback by a show of friendliness to respond. Some'll come around, and some won't. Either way just say: "Hi!" again tomorrow. And the day after that and the day after that. Don't think of it as doing *them* a favor—realize you're doing *yourself* one.

You see, when you stir authentic happiness into the mix, you progress beyond being positive—toward true *millionaire magnetism.* Now you are well on your way to being *a success magnet,* the flame that mesmerizes the moth, and once you've cracked that code, everything changes.

HOW TO ATTRACT SUCCESS

*Most people are about as happy as
they make up their minds to be.*

**Abraham Lincoln,
U.S. President**

In my rather unconventional book of Streetwise science, it seems logical to me that if positive attracts positive, transforming you into someone compelling and magnetic, then the opposite is also true: *negative attracts negative*. Worse still, negative doesn't simply attract negative, it *repels* positive, too. Ouch!

When you exude stress, worry, tension, anger, grumpiness, hate, superiority, arrogance, jealousy, or any other negative emotions, people won't be attracted to you. Simple as that. Instead of a success magnet, you'll be a success repellent!

Suze Ormond, a renowned personal finance guru, said something recently that struck a chord with me. She said something like, "Negative energy repels money." Makes a lot of sense to me; fits with my experiences and reflects the reality of what I see around me every day, from the streets to flash, brash Hollywood. After all, in order to manage wealth, you first have to be able to manage yourself.

If people like you, they'll want to do business with you

Do I believe luck happens to people? That some are luckier than others?

Well, I believe in good fortune. I feel pretty blessed myself, with my family, my health, and my life in general. But the truth is, luck is about being the right person in the right place at the right time— and that usually happens *by intent rather than accident*. It happens by harvesting seeds already sowed, following a breadcrumb trail already laid down, and by being, in effect, an accomplished self-marketer.

When I was a youngster, sittin' around the house wasn't an

option. Even if I wanted to, Dad would kick me out into the streets. He didn't even like me hangin' around the block, mixing with the neighborhood kids. "What good will that do you?" he'd ask. "Get your ass out there and see what else is goin' on. Meet some new faces. Put yourself around, son."

And that's just what I did. I was everywhere. Out and about—sometimes for days and nights—without break. I thought nothing of hoppin' a plane to L.A. or drivin' to Florida at a moment's notice. I never partied for the sake of partying, but I did party to get face recognition. People would see me in Chicago one day, Miami the next. They'd see me at this event and that event. I'd be at industry gigs, private parties, awards shows, big-fight nights in Vegas and New York. I made thousands of connections, hundreds of acquaintances, and a few good friends, too.

The result? Today I know people coast to coast, from all walks of life, and when the phone rings out of the blue with a new client or an unexpected invitation to someone's home for the weekend, it's not the result of luck, but of effort and intent.

Of course, it's no good just puttin' yourself out there if people don't want to associate with you. You gotta have the other critical piece of the equation right as well: you've got to be someone people want to be seen with and spend time with. It sure helps, then, if you have a great attitude and great personal style. We'll talk more about how critical these are to achieving personal, sustainable success.

Success, as we know, attracts more success. Success makes you magnetic. If that looks lucky then, man, you best run with it! It's pretty hard to separate success and happiness, seeing as they're so closely entwined, but even so, most of us get it the wrong way around. "If I'm successful," we say, "I'll be happy." Well, it's even simpler than that. *Be happy and success will follow.*

When you exude cheerfulness, people will want to know who you are and what you're all about. They'll think they're missing something and will want to be associated with you. Strangers will approach you in the street. Women will talk to you at parties. You'll stand out at work and shine socially. Don't believe me? Read the story of how I met my wife.

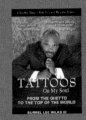

FREEWAY FREEFALL

I met my wife on the freeway.

I was exiting Route 94, veering onto Ohio, the sharply curved slip road that would take me into downtown Chicago, and home. It was about 7:30 in the evening, warm with the promise of summer just around the corner. I was tired and preoccupied.

This little silver bullet of a car came from behind and shot past on the inside lane, unceremoniously jerking me back to the present. Side by side, we each hugged the curve too tightly, then in a blur, she was gone. It took a split second. In that moment, I caught a glimpse of the woman who would become my wife.

How did I get her to stop? Well I put my foot down and, at the first set of traffic lights we came to, pulled up parallel, wound down my window, and attempted to strike up a conversation. At first, she resisted, pointedly ignoring me and keeping her eyes firmly fixed ahead. I repeated the process at the next three sets of lights. There was no shaking me. Maybe it was my perseverance or perhaps it was my smile, but whatever the reason, that little silver car pulled into the curbside behind me, as we entered the downtown area. —From *Tattoos on My Soul*

YA GOTTA **DO IT**

BE A SUCCESS MAGNET

So now you know the power of your thoughts, both positive and negative. If you're like most folks, you're so used to thinking negative thoughts, it's become a bad habit—something you do without even realizing it. Take the time to pay attention and really listen to the dialogue going on inside your head. The next time you catch yourself thinking negatively, visualize a big, red STOP sign. Then, flip the script, and picture the exact same topic or scenario as a positive one. Help yourself break the cycle!

13

STREETWISE STRATEGY #5: BE A GIANT!

If I have seen further, it is by standing on the shoulders of giants.

Isaac Newton,
Physicist and Astronomer

I was initiated to the streets at a very early age, and as I worked my way through that academy, I came across some real *Giants*.

Take my dad: We had a volatile father-son relationship, but when I was a kid, like most boys, I thought he walked on water. Burrel Lee Wilks II was a neighborhood kingpin who'd built his own illicit business empire, and was turning over a great deal of cash for the longest while. I used to join him on his business trips around the neighborhood. Little Burrel sitting on Big Burrel's shoulders, I'd soak up his game like gravy.

Now, my dad was undoubtedly a manipulative man, with a hard streak, too, but let me tell you he understood the power of politics and the politics of power better than most anyone I've met. I was fascinated by the way my father, not a large man, was able to stand head and shoulders above the rest of the guys he mixed with; how he controlled conversations without dominating them; how he used words, silence, and body language to his best advantage; and how he masterfully orchestrated the group dynamics to get the results he wanted. My old man sure knew when to play and when to fold.

There's a lot about my dad I wouldn't emulate, but there's even more about him that I admire and love. He was a powerful teacher for this thirsty student.

Lessons from a Giant

Even more infamous and influential than my dad was my mentor Tony Accardo, the head of the Chicago Outfit, a guy who for twenty-five years ran the most notorious and feared crime syndicate in America. A man who had run with Capone himself many years before. Fascinatingly, it was this man, this career mobster, who was most responsible for my transition from street gang to legitimacy, from short-term scamming to sustainable success.

Tony consistently steered me away from the ghetto, encouraged me to think bigger and better, and dared me to strive to be a Giant. Yes, Giants may write their own rules, but they're smart enough to know that they're players in a much larger game.

Now I was a precocious kid, for sure—always decades older in experience than in actual years. Tony used to say I had an old soul as we walked the neighborhood together, talking, debating, and arguing. Remarkably, given his reputation as one of the most feared mobsters of recent generations, Tony was generous with this scrappy young kid, taking time to educate me about the world and show me an alternative way through it.

It was Tony who showed me I was in a different kind of prison.

It was Tony who refused to encourage me to do wrong but pushed me to realize my full potential.

It was Tony who gave me the catalyst I needed to claw out of the quicksand of the streets.

CONVERSATION WITH TONY

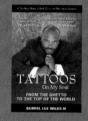

"Burrel, if I gave you the choice of being a big fish in a small pool in the ghetto," he said one day as we were circling the block on foot, "or a minnow in a bigger pond . . ." he stopped walking and turned to me. "What answer would you give me?"

It took me less than a second to respond. "A big fish," I said. "In fact, the biggest fish of all. I'm going be *king* of the West Side!"

Tony looked at me thoughtfully and resumed walking slowly. After a moment or two, he turned to me again and shook his head. "Wrong answer, kid. Wrong answer."

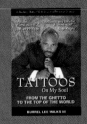

It took me a while to understand what Tony was talking about, and during the many hours across many years that we spent walking and talking, Tony did more than anyone to finally pry open my eyes and force me to see my life in a totally different light. But even as that light tentatively flickered on, I did everything within my power to turn it *off*. Self-awareness arrived slowly and painfully, my mind and internal survival mechanisms screaming *blue murder* at every glimmer that got through the blinds.

Insight is often unwelcome because with it comes responsibility. As a depressing consciousness of the ugliness, grubbiness, and "smallness" of my world seeped into me, it became tougher to ignore. Reluctantly, I began to open my mind to the possibility that there was a bigger apple out there and that I needed to take a bite of it.—From *Tattoos on My Soul*

DNA OF GIANTS: "MILLIONAIRE MAGNETISM"

Oh Lord it's hard to be humble
when you're perfect in every way.
I can't wait to look in the mirror
'cause I get better looking each day.

Mac Davis,
from "It's Hard to Be Humble"

We've all seen them on TV or in magazines. Maybe we've even bumped into one or two personally, in social or business circles. They're easy to spot because you feel the crackle of anticipation around them as they enter a room, commanding instant attention and leading entourages of admirers, who are hanging onto their every word as if they were gold coins from a slot machine. I'm referring to those individuals who seem to almost ooze confidence, success, and certainty. Those rare people who glow with *millionaire magnetism:* the Giants.

Who are they? Well, they're a diverse bunch to be sure. They come in many different packages. They might be as visibly famous and fabulously wealthy as Warren Buffet, Oprah Winfrey, or Tiger Woods; as compellingly charismatic as Dr. Martin Luther King Jr., Bill Clinton, or John Kennedy; as controversial as Frank Sinatra or Muhammad Ali; or as low key (but immensely powerful) as the Dalai Lama or Mother Teresa.

Giants have bottomless self-esteem. Their confidence shimmers around them like a force field, and instead of repelling, it attracts success, wealth, and, of course, *other* Giants. It takes only a split second for Giants to recognize one another. It's as though there's some kind of exclusive, virtual global club, and only the members know who they are.

It's easy to view Giants as if they're a different breed, born blessed with the right credentials or the right genes. It's easy to look at them from afar and wish you had just a fraction of their good fortune. But the truth is often far different. Giants may be born privileged, but more often they are as *everyman* as my friend Frank, who came from poverty and today owns an immense transportation business, or as *unassuming* as another friend Chris, who doesn't have two dimes to rub together but has the heart and presence of Goliath and a social agenda to change the world.

Fact is, you don't have to be born on the right side of the tracks to become a leader of stature. In fact, if you look closely enough, you'll find many folks who beat unbelievable personal odds to rise to the top. A Giant can even be that kid on the street corner, in the toughest part of town, fighting the social and economic currents that threaten to drown him, like a salmon swimming upstream, against all odds, on its way back home.

Savvy 7

RAGS TO RICHES

It isn't easy, but here in America, anyone has the right to achieve anything he or she wants. We've all heard Oprah's and Jewel's stories, seen Eminem's *8 Mile*, watched Shania Twain's *E! True Hollywood Story*, and celebrated the triumphs of many professional athletes and entertainers. But they're not the only ones. You might be surprised to learn the following people also scrapped their way out of modest backgrounds to become Giants.

1 Auto dealership legend Cal Worthington

2 Technology entrepreneur Bill Gates

3 Actors Mark and Donnie Walhberg

4 Cosmetics manufacturer Estée Lauder

5 Entertainment executive David Geffen

6 Broadcaster Larry King

7 Businessman and politician Ross Perot

BURREL'S SEVEN STREETWISE STRATEGIES

At home I am a nice guy:
but I don't want the world to know.
Humble people, I've found, don't get very far.

Muhammad Ali,
Boxing Heavyweight Champion of the World

Many Giants aren't even on the public stage. They don't enjoy operating in the glare of the spotlight. They value their privacy and, quietly and effectively, get on with the everyday business of success. *Gianthood* isn't something that can be "awarded" to you by a big job, paycheck, trust fund, or birthright. In fact, I know of a hundred sparrows with puffed out chests, hopping around self-importantly behind job titles and money. Well, a quick warning to all sparrows: you're living on borrowed glory and time, because authentic Gianthood is driven by what's inside, not the size of your expense account or wallet.

Remember, a Giant is never a bully,
and a bully never a Giant.
Scratch a loudmouth and you'll find a sparrow.

Burrel

WEALTHY-STRONG VERSUS WEALTHY-WEAK

I learned a long time ago that getting "money before sense" has no value at all and that "money without values" makes no sense at all.

Burrel

I spend a great deal of time hangin' with guys from the 'hood—but I also spend time in the inner circles of wealth. I mingle with artists, entertainers, and sports stars, and I work and socialize with wealthy businessmen, property developers, and entrepreneurs. It's fascinating to see how many of these folks are self-made, and how differently mature, hard-earned wealth expresses itself to the world versus the I-still-can't-believe-I've-got-all-this-money! kind of wealth.

Mature money is like a quiet conversation. Subtle, understated, totally self-confident, it seldom shouts because it doesn't feel the need to. The guys who have it don't wear their net worth on their sleeves; instead, they carefully tuck it away into their back pocket, where it multiplies and grows. This is about being *wealthy-smart* and *wealthy-strong.*

Brash-flash money, on the other hand, is more like a screaming match: loud, in-your-face, aggressive, and confrontational. It's showy and exhibitionist, flashy and fast-moving. This is disposable wealth— conspicuous consumption. Brash-flash money seldom grows, but it always flows. Usually all in one direction—out of your pocket and into someone else's! Trust me, it doesn't matter how much money you make, whether you earn twenty thousand bucks a year or twenty million: when it's gone, it's gone.

Too many people are stuck in the endless race of chasing *yesterday money* (money they've already spent) and *dream money* (the kind of cash they can only fantasize about), rather than *today money*—the kind that will take them into the future, and maybe even make some of those dreams come true.

Yup, we're so busy chasing the fantasy of the big bucks, that we

186

spend all of our *today money* on cars, big houses, bling, and exotic vacations to impress others into believing we've made it. Guess what? *Today money* borrowed on credit soon becomes *yesterday money*, and any chance of earning *dream money* slips further away from our grasp. Chasing yesterday money is exhausting and thankless. If anything will kill your dreams, this will. How can you look forward when your life is in hock, and debt and creditors are pulling you backward?

We need to steer clear of this poverty of ambition, where people want to drive fancy cars and wear nice clothes and live in nice apartments but don't want to work hard to accomplish these things. Everyone should try to realize their full potential.

**Barack Obama,
U.S. Senator**

I went through this learning curve myself as a young foolish guy. I earned millions as a bad street kid doing all the wrong things, but what I did next is not so different to what so many respectable, professional, white-collar folks do today: I squandered all my money on stuff I didn't need. I lost millions, by making stupid, reactive, materially driven decisions.

Don't get me wrong. I still love how "the other half" lives. I love wearing fine clothes and state-of-the-art-watches. I enjoy diamonds and magnificent cars. So no, don't get me wrong. I'm not advocating you hide your shine under a bushel of corn, but I *am* advising that, like me, you make sure that these material things aren't driving you, but that you're driving them.

So, yes, I'm a guy who likes a little flamboyance, a few diamonds, and a Rolls Royce or two. I like my outside to reflect my view of the world, my own personal brand if you like (and later in this chapter I'll explain more about the importance of creating a Personal Power Brand that radiates success). I dress well, in Zilli and Briony. I wear an Audemar Piguet watch and handmade shoes; but, these exterior trappings are simply a reflection of my character and style. They don't define it.

Flash and wealth can co-exist—just look at Diddy, J. Lo, and Donald Trump—but make no mistake, these guys understand money is just a means to an end. They make it work for them. This is what separates the wealthy-strong from the wealthy-weak. The wealthy-weak mistakenly believe that wealth defines them, and by doing so, they allow it to control them.

Giants know the true "value" of wealth.
They understand that it's simply a trading currency,
a means to an end, and that it can disappear as
fast—or even faster—than it arrived.

Burrel

Ah. I wasn't always this wise. I had to learn the hard way about the value of money, and how to separate the value of the cash from the value of the person. But learn I did.

Events of the past couple of years proved something that, my whole life, I'd understood intuitively and had observed time and again. Money that comes too easily never sticks around, and the wrong kind of money can never help you do the right kind of things. Like trying to hold water in your hands, it'll trickle clean through your fingers, before evaporating into nothingness.

I've seen a hundred ghetto-millionaires who, today, don't have two pennies to rub together, my father included. Most couldn't begin to tell you how they lost their fortunes. Like a homing pigeon, bad money will always find its way back from where it came—and in my experience, that's usually the streets.

Even fortunes earned the right way will fly out of the door a thousand times faster than they flew in. Money that has never earned respect, sure as hell won't give any in return. Look at some of the young entertainers out there today, making millions in moments and spending it twice as fast. These young kids can't imagine their gravy train ever running dry, and when it does, they've no place to go. Superstar or street hustler, it makes no difference when you're broke.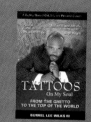

I've faced some harsh financial realities, but in the process, something extraordinary happened. I no longer defined myself by the magnitude of my wealth. I wore my cap to the wind. I knew that whatever I achieved, it would be down to my character, spirit, talent, and tenacity.

Now that felt good!—From *Tattoos on My Soul*

TOP 10 QUALIFICATIONS FOR GIANTHOOD

A leader takes people where they want to go.
A great leader takes people where they don't necessarily
want to go, but ought to be.

Rosalynn Carter,
First Lady

The Language of Giants

These young guys are playing checkers.
I'm out there playing chess.

Kobe Bryant,
Professional Basketball Player

Have you noticed, when you are in the presence of Giants, you somehow feel smaller? Well, this is no accident. Giants intuitively know how to take command. Leadership is practically second nature to them. Next time you're in a room with a Giant, pay close attention to some of the following characteristics—and then work on emulating them yourself.

1. **Giants have unshakable self-belief:** It's impossible to be a real chief without self-esteem. Some folks are born with an unwavering sense of their own worth (me included!), but others have to work hard (as Oprah did) to cultivate self-confidence. You may have to reprogram ingrained thought patterns—patterns that have been there since you were a child—but you can and must because Giants use their certainty like jet-propulsion.

2. **Giants are Mind Jedis:** "I am because I say I am." Giants understand the power of their minds. They know if they can

dream it, they can be it, and if they imagine something vividly enough, it will become real soon enough.

3. **Giants never ask permission, nor make excuses:** You don't need anyone's "say-so" except your own, and true Giants share one of the biggest secrets of all—they know that they are the *permission givers.* Giants write their own rule books and understand that "success requires no explanation, and failure allows no alibi."

4. **They are risk takers and opportunity makers:** "The biggest mistakes are the mistakes of omission, not commission," said Warren Buffet. In other words, it's not what you do, but what you don't that will slow you down. Giants know they'll hurt themselves more by *not trying* than by *trying and failing.* Giants are market makers. They'll see an opportunity and go all out for it, brushing away failure like gnats on a hot summer day!

5. **Giants don't acknowledge boundaries:** Boundaries are constraints created in our own minds. Social and economic hierarchy, race, gender, and education are all "artificial" boxes that many are all too ready to jump into. Giants don't need to climb over these walls. They don't even see them.

6. **Giants are relentless:** They know that outer strength comes from inner discipline. They have tenacity, staying power, determination, and steadiness. Giants can move mountains through force of will and sheer persistence.

7. **Giants have endless optimism:** Even bad situations can become positive, when you believe that every "no" is taking you one step closer to "yes" and that what doesn't kill you only makes you stronger.

Eagles don't flock; you have to find them one at a time.

Ross Perot,
Business Executive and Political Leader

8. **Giants zig when everyone else zags:** Frankly, Giants don't give a damn what anyone else thinks. When I was younger, I caused a stir by going my own way, doing my own thing, and creating my own style. If everyone headed east, I'd be goin' west. Before long, thinkin' they were missin' out on something, they'd all turn around to follow me. Giants embrace their individuality and are usually ahead of the crowd.

9. **Giants always "keep it real":** There is little bullshit in the world of chiefs. They've simply got no time for it. My personal promise of "life coaching without sugarcoating" reflects that philosophy. Giants cut right to the chase, hate fakes, and usually give a guy only one chance to get it right.

10. **Giants are mostly "self-made":** Vince Lombardi said, "Leaders aren't born; they are made. And they are made just like anything else, through hard work. And that's the price we all have to pay to achieve that goal, or any goal."

I pretty much approach every season never thinking about what I accomplished the year before.

Jerry Rice,
Professional Football Player

DEVELOP THE BODY LANGUAGE OF A GIANT

Kinetics is the science of body language, and your body language, without question, will reveal whether you're a player or a wannabe. Study and adopt these seven tips, and you'll take command of any room you enter.

1 Occupy your space like you mean it. Go ahead and take the seat at the head of the table, or the passenger front seat, deferring only when it would be rude not to do so. Don't shrink into your chair or wind your legs around it.

2 Sit with good posture. Shoulders down and back, chest up, chin level, spine erect. Don't slouch.

3 Stand with good posture, too. Don't cock your hip to one side and put most of your weight on one foot. Instead, distribute your weight between both feet equally.

4 Breathe evenly and deeply. It will help you remain calm in a stressful situation and make you appear confident and in control.

5 Use the steeple hand position, which leaders frequently assume during meetings or when speaking to a crowd. Touch the tip of each finger to the tip of the corresponding finger on the other hand, with fingers spread.

6 Don't touch your face, head, or neck while you talk. Keep your hands on your lap or use them to gesture your point.

7 SMILE!

CREATE YOUR PERSONAL POWER BRAND

*You have to learn to be a Master Marketer and treat
yourself like a premium brand.*

Burrel

The way we package, present, and project ourselves has a direct impact on how successful we'll be. When I was a kid, I instinctively knew I was my own best asset, and that I should package myself in a manner that declared my status as a leader. I was fortunate to be nudged along the way by a couple of savvy—and stylish—mentors.

Tony Accardo, the classically and exquisitely tailored Chicago mobster, used to laugh at the glitz and glamor of my diamonds and designer clothes, but he respected my individuality. And though our styles may have differed, we each understood the one simple, nonnegotiable rule I've been repeating from the start of this book: success attracts success.

I want you to write this down, scorch it onto your heart, burn it onto your brain:

*If you want to get on in life, you have to look as
though you've already arrived.*

Burrel

Even as you are working on your "inside" transformation, don't forget that one of the most effective ways to change people's perceptions toward you is to repackage what's on the *outside*. Building a strong image is one of the best power plays you can make. If you want to be a winner, then you have to think like a winner, act like a winner, and look like a winner. There're no prizes in this life for gray or vanilla. So, my friends, it's time to go Technicolor! It's time to shine.

BURREL'S SEVEN STREETWISE STRATEGIES

A brand for a company is like a reputation for a person. You earn reputation by trying to do hard things well.

**Jeff Bezos,
Founder of Amazon.com**

REAL TALK

My man Ron sat in front of me, looking like an overstuffed sofa, and a garage sale one at that. He was a big man, standing six-foot-three and weighing in at around three hundred pounds. Under his wrinkled sports coat was a shirt practically busting at the seams, its pearl buttons doing their darndest to restrain his enormous belly. I'm not lying when I say that shirt made me nervous—I kept waiting for one of those buttons to fly off and take out my eye! But Ron didn't care. He sat there with that confident presence only big dudes usually have, leaning back in his chair, hands clasped behind his head. So what did he need from me?

"I'm a successful man, Burrel. I can afford the better things in life." Ron smiled sheepishly, patted his giant gut, then looked serious again. "But I've let myself go. Face it, I look like a slob, I can't keep a woman, and, to be honest, I'm not sure I'll live to see fifty."

He continued, explaining that he'd spent the last decade building his business empire, and while he'd had his nose to the grindstone, the world had changed. He and his ex-wife had split up almost nine years ago, and though he'd been out with women since, he didn't fit into the L.A. dating scene. You see, he'd put all his energy into his professional life, while ignoring his personal life. He was a successful man, but he was lonely and unhappy.

Man, if only all my clients were as motivated as Ron! He was already dead set on making some changes, so I set him up with a top-notch personal trainer, and he got right to work. Over a period of a few months, we focused on building Brand Ron: the sophisticated, stylish entrepreneur. We strengthened both his body and his mind, improved his self-confidence and social skills, and created a unique style that was all his own.

I taught Ron that in order to attract the kind of woman he was looking for, he needed to be the flame, not the moth. Plus, Ron had a tendency to get too caught up in his emotions too early with women—he had to learn to start relationships with a healthy mix of head and heart. Now, Ron was a successful dude when I met him, but today he's successful and happy. He's not as round as he used to be, having replaced his belly with a well-rounded life instead. Ron met a fantastic lady about eight months ago, and he and Laura are headed toward marriage.

And best of all, I have no doubt Ron will live a long and healthy life!

Of course, creating a compelling personal image isn't something that you can treat as a part-time job. Your image isn't defined only by how you dress, where you socialize, or what you wear to the office each day. An image isn't something you put on in the morning and take off at night. It runs deeper than that and is a reflection of your behavior and character as well as your clothes. Yup, designing an enduring, effective image takes more than slapping on a new suit. It takes *real commitment*.

BUILDING A PERSONAL POWER BRAND

*Remember always that you not only have the right to be
an individual, you have an obligation to be one.*

**Eleanor Roosevelt,
First Lady**

There are practical reasons why you need to stand out from the crowd: reasons such as attracting a partner, improving job security, or taking advantage of promotional opportunities. I mean, with all the economic uncertainty today, competition in the job market, and a rapidly changing, technology-enabled world that offers little in the way of predictability or stability, you've gotta find ways to *differentiate* yourself, to stand out from the masses.

Say there's buzz about a promotion in the air; well, who's more likely to get it? Will it be Steady Sam, the nice guy who works quietly and obediently at his desk all day, or you, Dynamic Dan, packaged and presented as the confident, smart company asset that you are?

Once you view your personal branding strategy as *both defense and offense,* you understand that taking care of yourself, dressing right, and staying groomed and cool is not self-indulgence—it's good business.

So where the heck do you start?

Well, branding is nothing new, so why don't you learn from the champions? Believe it or not, you can learn from all those products, competing for your attention on crowded supermarket shelves. Yup, you'll learn as much about personal branding from Coca-Cola as you will from Martha Stewart or Michael Jordan.

You see, each of us is a *brand,* and *brand status*—whether we become a market leader or a "me-too product"—all depends on how well we separate ourselves from the pack, and how effectively we present, package, and market our assets. Think of yourself as a *corporation of one:* the boss of a business enterprise called YOU.

Okay, many of you are probably familiar with Marketing 101, so

197

you know that in order to effectively market a product, you need a product that is: 1) high quality, 2) available in the right place (and time), 3) set at the right price, and 4) appealingly packaged and promoted. Well *human brands* aren't so very different.

- **Product:** You are the product, and you should be substantial, strong, and positive. You should bring value to those who "buy" you. What is it about you that's special, different, and valuable? Are you thorough, quick, mathematically inclined, or artistic? Are you kind, thoughtful, funny, or intuitive? *Identify your best assets.* They are what you're going to be "selling."

- **Place:** If we're to be successful, we need to be "available" for success. So "place" is all about your *accessibility*. If you don't circulate with the right folks, and you don't get the face recognition in the right places, how are you going to find a "buyer"? Like I've said before, luck happens when you put yourself in its path, and like it or not, "lady luck" is generally an extrovert. Like her, you've gotta be out and about in order to know what opportunities are out and about, too.

In what kind of places should you hang out? Best believe, you will be measured by the company you keep. Not buying it? I saw a research study a while ago that was pretty convincing. Some market researchers had shown a bunch of folks a picture of a pretty white dress that had been featured in a number of different magazines and newspapers. They asked how much people thought that dress cost. Now the ones who saw the dress in *Vogue* magazine automatically assumed it would be as expensive and classy as the magazine it was featured in. They estimated it would cost thousands of dollars. But when people saw it featured in the local newspaper—the same exact picture of the same exact dress—sitting alongside ads for used cars and grocery store coupons, they thought it must be cheap, too, and assumed it would only cost something like twenty bucks! Remember, much of marketing is built on perception.

- **Price:** None of us have a price stamped on our foreheads, do we? I sure hope not anyhow. When I look at "price" in the context of Personal Power Brands, I think of whether we're viewed as being of *high value* or *low value*. None of us wants to be seen as "cheap" like the dress in the newspaper ads, but in order be seen as "premium," we must sell the perception of being better than the rest. Why do people pay more for a bottle of Coke than for Wal-Mart's own brand cola—even if they think both drinks taste pretty much the same? Because of Coca-Cola's branding, we trust its product, believe it tastes better, and is worth paying a premium for. You gotta decide: do you want to be a premium brand or strictly a "generic" label?

- **Packaging and Promotion:** This is something we all intuitively understand but often neglect. When you picked up that can of Coke, you'd already made a brand decision. You were attracted to its great packaging, and you love the ads, too. Keep that firmly in mind as you begin to "package" yourself.

The expression of your brand offer is called *brand positioning*.

Consider Fred, a successful guy by many standards: well-educated, respected, and appreciated as a solid contributor by his company, as evidenced by his slow but steady rise through the ranks. Everyone knew you could bank on Fred. But in many ways, Fred had become just another of the company fixtures and was being taken for granted.

It was time to shake things up and reposition Fred. We started by focusing on how he would like to be perceived, not only by work colleagues, but also by the folks he mixed with socially. What image did Fred need to project?

How about: "Fred Alvarez: The Totally Dependable Guy"?

Hmm. This was close to how Fred was seen today and was neither compelling, nor remotely sexy!

Okay, let's try: "Alfred Alvarez: Stanford Educated Innovator."

Now that's more like it. Short, to the point, and it says everything. I mean, we automatically assume that innovators are dynamic, energizing, forward-thinking, inventive, inspiring, and exciting. So in that one simple *tag-line* we move Fred from being seen as a solid "plodder" into a force to be reckoned with. The best tag-lines in the world are the ones that simply sum up the promise of the brand.

So, what do you want people to say about you?

Look at the following positioning statements and see how they work for these products:

- BMW: The Ultimate Driving Machine (this speaks for itself)

- Apple: Think Different (innovative, unique, individual)

- Nike: Just Do It (empowering, energizing, inspiring)

Now, think for a moment: what would be your brand positioning statement, if you had to create one for yourself?

Think of it this way: You show up at a small cocktail party where only the host knows you. Still, you chat with everyone, taking an authentic interest in your fellow party-goers, and then leave the room to take a phone call. Everyone immediately turns to your host and asks: who is that guy?

Your host smiles, looks mysterious, and says:

"Oh, that's YOUR NAME HERE.

He's_____!"

Now you go ahead and fill in the blanks!

Savvy7

NOW YOU'RE STYLIN'!

Style isn't about designer labels, it's about HOW you wear your clothes. Follow these tips to develop your own original and powerful sense of style.

1 It doesn't matter if a particular style is splashed across the pages of every magazine. If it doesn't look good on your body type, it won't look good on you. Figure out which pieces look best on you, and build your wardrobe around them.

2 If you want to be taken seriously, don't be a slave to trends. Trends are for teenagers. Style is for adults.

3 Spend money on good, quality pieces. Every adult should own a leather jacket or blazer, a quality pair of dress shoes, well-made slacks that fit, a well-fitting pair of jeans, and, of course, a great suit. Spend less on trendy fashions.

4 For god's sake, people, buy yourself a respectable watch already!

5 Ladies, you don't need to spend $10,000 on a designer purse, but you should own a good one. If you're still carrying a kitschy, cutesy purse anywhere besides a child's birthday party, it's time to invest in a bag that announces your intentions to be taken seriously. Outlet malls are a good source for discounts on reputable brands such as Coach or Dooney & Bourke. You can even "rent" designer bags at sites such as www.bagborroworsteal.com. Fellas, same thing goes for your wallet. Velcro wallets are for boys, not men.

6 Donald Trump can get away with a horrible hairstyle, but you can't. Maybe you can't afford the hottest salon in town, but you can afford a regular haircut. Ponytails and ball caps don't say you mean business.

Savvy7

7 Toss out clothing that is worn, stained, snagged, or out of style. If your favorite shirt has a stain on it, find another favorite shirt. Wearing old, worn-out clothing says you don't care about yourself, so why should anybody else?

DRESS FOR SUCCESS

Style is knowing who you are, what you want to say, and not giving a damn.

**Gore Vidal,
Novelist and Essayist**

All Personal Power Brands have four qualities that add up to a high-value, attractive proposition. They are:

- **Distinctive:** My own "positioning" is a good example of this. I am: "America's Most Authentic Life Coach!" You know exactly what to expect from me.

- **Differentiated:** There's no one else out there offering my trademark: "Life Coaching Without Sugarcoating."

- **Relevant:** Make sure your positioning fits your goals. Being "Dependable Fred" is unlikely to work, if you're interviewing with a new high-tech start-up or trying to impress a hot date.

- **Consistent:** Once you've developed your personal positioning make sure your behavior, style and the things and people you surround yourself with are a consistent reflection of how you wish to be perceived.

Let's talk for a moment about style, because a great many people confuse style with fashion. John Fairchild, of *Women's Wear Daily*, says, "Style is an expression of individualism mixed with charisma. Fashion is something that comes after style."

Create your own visual style . . . let it be unique for yourself and yet identifiable for others.

**Orson Welles,
Actor and Director**

REAL TALK

RÉSUMÉ ON YOUR WRIST!

As much as I love fine automobiles, you can't take 'em with you on planes or into restaurants. But that's okay, because I'm gonna let you in on a little secret: when you're making a first impression, people aren't going to be looking at your car, or your house, or the bills in your wallet. You might not realize it, but your *watch* lets people quickly determine whether you're a true player or a wannabe!

Now, we all know first impressions are formed within a New York second—you're bagged and tagged, and if your packaging is shabby, you'll be relegated to bargain bin status, along with last year's holiday cards.

The quickest way to pass the "scan test" is to flash your player ID—a watch that makes a statement. No kiddin'. A quality watch will say more about you in a matter of seconds than a résumé or sales presentation could even begin to cover.

I don't really care what people think . . .
I just do my own thing. . . . I like being loud and
letting people know I'm there.

James Brown,
Singer and Songwriter

YA GOTTA **DO IT**

BE A GIANT!

If you want to get on in life, you have to look as though you've already arrived. Now, I don't recommend maxing out your credit cards buying a closet full of new designer clothes. But you must dress like you mean business, every single day. Take a couple of hours to go through your closet and dresser drawers. Remove everything that doesn't fit, is faded, has stains or tears, or is old and hopelessly out of style. You're better off wearing the same sharp, memorable outfit every day than a whole truckload of ill-fitting, cheap, and/or worn clothing.

14

STREETWISE STRATEGY #6: SEPARATE THE EMOTIONAL FROM THE FINANCIAL

Avoid having your ego so close to your position that when your position falls, your ego goes with it.

Colin Powell,
Secretary of State

Emotion can mess up everything. It clouds judgment, muddies our ability to be objective and clear, and forces us to do things that we sometimes regret for the rest of our lives. If you can learn how to separate yourself emotionally from a situation, then you're well on your way to becoming a *master strategist,* the button pusher, the puppet master rather than the fool jerking around on the end of a string!

When I talk about separating the *emotional* from the *financial,* I mean that you always have to keep a clear head and see the bigger picture. And remember, you may have to lose a few battles to win the war. You see, too many of us react to situations as though someone else wrote the script, and we're just mouthing the lines. *Real* power lies in writing your own lines, not parroting someone else's.

Let me give you an example.

You have to make a presentation to a major client, who just happens to be a real you-know-what. You hate dealing with him, 'cause you know he's going to put you down in front of everyone. He's done it before. Last time you met him, he was flat-out rude and could barely sit still while you presented. He alternated between looking at his watch and playing with his cell phone, then he abruptly stood up and walked out of the room in the middle of your presentation, leaving you feeling like an ass! To top it all, this idiot is about ten years younger than you.

He made you look foolish, and naturally enough, you felt defensive, even angry.

And, of course, that was exactly his plan. Here's a guy who gets off on flexing his *authority muscles.* He's nothing more than a schoolyard bully in a suit. So you now have two choices: play the game his way and fight on the playground, or *change* the rules.

Remember how we talked earlier about arming yourself with *magnetic attitude,* and how by doing so you can eliminate the negative? Well, here's your chance to test that theory.

Meet his *negative* energy with nothing but *positive* force. Make sure your face and body language are open. Move around the room toward him, shake his hand, look him in the eye, and let him know with a big smile, what a pleasure it is to meet him again!

Present warmly and openly. Don't let his vibe intimidate you. Don't get defensive. Respond to questions and comments with crisp, positive, and confident energy. And make sure that your body language isn't sending a different message. Keep your head up, your shoulders back, and your hands expressive. Make sure your smile reaches your eyes (think of something warm and nice when you smile, like your kids, your dog, or your team winning the Super Bowl).

Let him carry on with his childish game playing. Don't allow him to get under your skin. You're standing in front of him as a player bringing some great things to the table, things that will benefit him and his business. That's your position, and you're not going to allow him to position you any other way.

Kill him with kindness.

Now folks, you gotta trust me on this one. Guys like him are a dime a dozen in the 'hood. I've faced countless situations where if the deal turns sour, it might turn deadly. It may seem weak to smile in the face of adversity, but best believe, it will throw guys like this (and women, I know they're out there, too) for a loop.

And, don't forget those visualization techniques we talked about earlier. Imagine him as your elderly auntie, who is a bit senile and needs handling with extra patience. Or visualize yourself as a red-hot heat source, flames poppin' and crackin', slowly melting his frigid shell into a puddle.

Now you've turned the tables.

Remember if you consistently exude warmth and self-confidence, he'll either respond positively (remember, positive attracts positive, and guys like this respect people who don't back down), or continue to act like a jerk. And if that's the case, he'll end up looking like a jackass! Most likely, you're not the only one in the boardroom who's turned off by his juvenile behavior. Flip the script on the situation and even if you don't win him over, you'll have impressed everybody else in the room.

You may not close the sale, and he may still have been a pain. He may even have shredded you, yet again, loudly and publicly, but you did *not* allow him to back you into a corner. You played against *the game*, not against *him*, and, in doing so, you won a great personal victory.

Darrell was a successful guy, the owner of two furniture stores he built from the ground up. But he was about to lose it all when he came to me about his right-hand man, Tony.

See, Darrell is the soul of the business. His vision, years of hard work, and money made those stores. He's got an eye for design and a way with top-flight clients that have earned him the opportunity to furnish the most expensive homes in the city.

Tony came on board a few years ago and brought with him the operational experience Darrell sorely needed. He knew how to run a profitable retail store, deal with employees, and save the company money by making better deals with new suppliers and distributors.

Yeah, Darrell was willing to admit that Tony was an important part of the business. But the point was, it wasn't just a business, it was *his* business! So when Tony had the nerve to ask Darrell for an equal partnership, Darrell got mad. Real mad.

It was a dangerous stalemate. Tony was threatening to leave and probably would take a few good employees and clients with him. Darrell resented Tony for pressuring him and would rather close the whole damn thing down than budge an inch.

What a stupid waste that would be. Just think of all those years of hard work, all the equity in that profitable business, and the break up of one heck of a good team—all gone to waste because ego and emotion trumped good ol' common sense.

I taught Darrell that business decisions—especially financial ones—require objective thinking. Emotions get in the way of objective decision making and must **REAL TALK** be kept in check. Now true, Tony shouldn't have come at Darrell that way, asking for half, then resorting to threats when he didn't get what he wanted, but once Darrell calmed down and looked at the situation objectively, he realized Tony was responsible for pretty much all of the day-to-day operations. And his efficiency measures had increased profits, not to mention giving Darrell more free time. Darrell approached Tony to patch up their differences, and the two hammered out a deal that gave Tony full partnership, but also required that he assume greater accountability for production and profitability.

They've already opened a new store and have plans for three more. Now can you imagine throwing all that away over emotions and pride?

I know I sound like a broken record, but I repeat it because it's so important to understand this about human nature: whatever plays out on the streets, plays out, too, in boardrooms and homes across America, every single day. All the strutting, posturing, and testosterone you see on street corners is also strutting its way around offices, factories, and living rooms across the world. Yup, bullying, ego battles, personal conflict, and the general pushin' and shovin' for power and control is, unfortunately, part of everyday life. If you can separate yourself emotionally from a situation, you're already head and shoulders above most people out there, who respond with a kind of mechanical knee-jerk whenever someone presses their buttons.

You ever hear the story about a frog and a scorpion crossing a flooded stream? The scorpion persuades the frog to carry him across the river on his back, but halfway across, the scorpion stings the frog, and they both begin to drown. "Why?" asks the stricken frog. "Now we'll both die!"

The scorpion replies simply, "It's my nature."

There are many folks who, like that scorpion, would rather drown than change their ways. And unlike you or I, they will always be wannabes. Never winners.

MANAGING CONFLICT LIKE A MASTER

Holding onto anger is like grasping a hot coal
with the intent of throwing it at someone else;
you are the one who gets burned.

Buddha,
Philosopher and Religious Leader

As a life coach, I get called upon often to mediate conflict with col-leagues, family, business associates, even neighbors. These highly charged exchanges are often sparked by some small, apparently inconsequential event. The neighbor's dog barking again. The guy who thinks his girl was flirting with his best friend. A bust-up with a teenage son who stayed out too late. A perceived slight at work. The small, but potentially dangerous irritations that happen pretty much every day. In reality, though, most fights are far from spontaneous, and come about from tension that has been brewing for a while.

It only takes a single spark of irritation to ignite pent-up resentment and cause one heck of an emotional explosion! Weeks, months, even years of unspoken bitterness can bubble to the surface like hot oil, hiss-ing and spitting all over the place. The argument grows until pretty much *everyone* has lost sight of what it was about in the first place.

What should have been an easy answer turns into all-out war. Soon lines are drawn between sides, words spoken that can't be tak-en back, threats made, and possibly blows landed. It's a mess, but no one's going to give ground for fear they'll lose face and respect. Everyone loses.

Most direct conflict is totally avoidable. You can learn how to side-step it or defuse it. Here are some pointers:

- **Recognize your "danger zones":** These are words or situations that set off the emotional firecrackers! It could be the way your boss or wife looks at you (you know *the look*), or a certain tone of voice someone uses, or a dismissive gesture, or a certain way of criticizing. Or perhaps you get defensive when you're tired, stressed out, hungry, or had one drink too many. The point is: once you recognize the patterns, you can identify your *danger zones,* spot 'em coming, and create a diversion!

- **Learn not to sweat the small stuff:** Life *isn't* fair. Stuff will happen. Don't dwell on past grievances—learn from them and move on. And don't forget what we said earlier in this book: learn how to see each and every day as *a lesson or a blessin'.* Changing the way you view your world will allow you to see opportunities in obstacles, and duck conflict when it rears its head.

> *The most extraordinary thing about the oyster is this. Irritations get into the shell . . . And when he cannot get rid of them, he uses the irritations to do the loveliest thing an oyster ever has the chance to do. If there are irritations in our lives today, there is only one prescription: make a pearl.*
> **Harry Emerson Fosdick,**
> **Theologian**

> *That's kind of how I approach life and football; why dwell on something that hasn't happened?*
> **Brett Favre,**
> **NFL Legend**

- **Listen first:** Go beyond hearing only the words; try to understand what the other person is actually *saying.* Listen carefully to them, instead of thinking about what you're going to say next. Take time to process and consider their words; try to feel the emotion they are trying to convey. Active listening is a skill that requires concentration and patience.

- **Think before you speak:** Consciously hold back your words until your brain has engaged, and ban yourself from saying anything *negative.* Make sure your words and tone aren't angry, defensive, accusatory, or sarcastic. By the way, the same principle applies to e-mail. Never respond in anger to any written communication, either. Whenever you feel anger bubbling to the surface, or hear yourself mentally rehearsing an angry, negative response in your head, STOP! Count to ten and breath deeply (yes, it really does work).

- **Watch your body language:** When you walk down a street on Chicago's West Side at night, you'd better know what's going down unless you want to walk straight into trouble. Your body language, the way you walk, your facial expressions, your nervousness, whether you're sweating or not, and, above all, the wrong kind of eye contact can all get you into deep water. It's vital you understand the *language of the streets*. The same principle applies in every other situation, too. Don't only talk with your mouth. Talk with your whole body. Sometimes we think we're saying one thing, while our body language is screaming something contradictory. And the loudest voice of all is our eyes: those "windows to the soul" that give us away every time. Never forget, your eyes tell the whole story, so you'd better make sure they're transmitting the right one!

- **Flip the script.** We talked about this earlier in Hustle with Heart. Simply put, it means: "do the unexpected." There's no better way to defuse conflict than by completely screwing with your opponent's head. And I don't mean that in a bad way. Most of us are conditioned to react to certain triggers, and those reactions are usually *predictable*. So you must do the unpredictable to regain advantage. He expects you to be upset, so smile. She expects to see anger and frustration, so give her optimism and positivity.

In times of great stress or adversity, it's always best to keep busy; to plow your anger and your energy into something positive.

**Lee Iacocca,
Automotive Industry Leader**

THE POWER OF WORDS

Expecting life to treat you well because you are a good person is like expecting an angry bull not to charge because you are a vegetarian.

Shari R. Barr,
Author

What if you can't avoid conflict, and you are left with no choice but to navigate your way through it? What's the best strategy to adopt? Can you kill violence with silence? Walking away from conflict can be a powerful weapon, but *silence* can be *two-faced.* You see, silence, more often than not, can be used as another form of aggression. Men and women the world over have mastered the art of slyly using silence as a weapon.

If you've ever received the cold shoulder, or been excluded from conversations or closed out of friendships, then you've been a victim. But if you've ever used glares, exasperated sighs, or stomping feet to make your own point, or if you've ever turned your back in silent disgust on your partner at bedtime, then you've been an *antagonist,* too. Let's face it: there's really no such thing as *true silence,* because even when your mouth is shut, your body will be talking, loud and clear as a bell.

Disassociating from a conflict situation can work, but it will probably only delay the inevitable. To resolve conflict, you must be prepared to be clear, calm, objective, but engaged. In the end, there is no substitute for the right words, used wisely.

Wise men talk because they have something to say; fools, because they have to say something.

Plato,
Philosopher

Words: clever, persuasive, humorous, and sincere. Oh, yes, words are powerful, something I understood even as a *shorty.* I like to use 'em, too, lots of 'em! Heck, I make my living with words, and when it comes to any kind of conflict, mobilizing words is my strategy of choice. I will always (unless someone I cared for was bodily threatened) choose to be a negotiator rather than a warrior, a mediator rather than a fighter, a persuader rather than an enforcer.

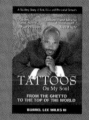

> Words and force of personality were *my* weapons of choice, my bullets. And highly effective they were, too. I was the mouth, the *Muhammad Ali,* of Cicero: mediating, cajoling, haranguing, persuading, and threatening. I rarely came up for air once on a roll. With my verbal armory fully deployed, a man might feel as though he were in front of a firing squad! Capitulation was common.
> —From *Tattoos on My Soul*

Too many youngsters are pressured by bullies to do things they don't want to do, or be something they don't want to be, and too often, they can't see a way out of the situation. They still have to go to school each day, walk down the street, live in the same neighborhood. They become fearful, start skippin' school, and duckin' out of sight. I recently gave a youngster this advice: "Look that bully in the eye and tell him that you need to stay in school because you plan on being an attorney, and one day he's gonna need you, and you plan on helpin' him for free." On this occasion, it was a strategy that worked, but if it hadn't, we would have tried something else. We would have kept using *words to fend off fists.*

So I teach youngsters, and a lot of older folks who should know better than to be fighting in the first place, how to defuse conflict with a few choice words. I teach them when to hold and when to fold, how to flip the script with some unexpected verbals, and when to use words as a torrent or trickle. I also explain how to *kill violence with silence,* by simply turning and walking away. But the main lesson

I keep drumming in? *Engaging your brain and mouth is always going to trump engaging your trigger finger.* Yup. If you can master verbal weaponry, you're already the winner.

> *Am I not destroying my enemies*
> *when I make friends of them?*
>
> **Abraham Lincoln,**
> **U.S. President**

REAL TALK   Okay, friends, pay attention to this story. My man Russell did what lots of people do: he used mental visualization in a negative way and paid the price.

See, Russell felt he was being denied a promotion at work because his boss, Jeff, had it in for him. It was clear from day one that the guy just didn't like him. He was constantly picking on him, pointing out every little thing he did wrong and giving him all the crap assignments. Russell worked hard and brought in great numbers, but Jeff got all the credit.

Russell didn't ask Jeff what the problem was; instead, he figured the dude was jealous. After all, Russell was young and bright, a real up-and-comer. He'd fast-tracked into the lead position on his team and had even been picked to give a presentation at the annual meeting last year, which had given him visibility with the higher-ups. He was simply a threat to Jeff.

Russell stewed over what he perceived as Jeff's slights, until he became a man obsessed. He mentally rehearsed the showdown he would have with Jeff. He memorized all the clever things to say, things that would really piss off Jeff. He'd show him!

And then, inevitably, Russell got into a shouting match **REAL** with Jeff, and all those scathing words he'd mentally TALK practiced over and over poured out of him in a flood of white-hot rage. Then, as it had played out a hundred times in his head, Russell walked right out that door. And right out of his job.

You see, because Russell had rehearsed the showdown so many times, it was easy to make it real. Problem was, Russell didn't use the power of mental movies to achieve his goals and dreams; he used it to achieve a *moment's satisfaction.* And I know Russell would agree when I tell you the satisfaction he got from telling off the boss lasted only one night as he drank *waaaay* too much and bored his friends, then the entire bar, with slurred retellings of his moment of triumph. By morning, the short-lived victory was an embarrassing memory, and Russell was looking for a new job.

YA GOTTA **DO IT**

SEPARATE THE EMOTIONAL FROM THE FINANCIAL

It's difficult to control automatic emotional responses such as the urge to cry or get angry; however, one bodily response we CAN control is our breathing. And breathing can actually help you control your emotions! The next time you feel yourself becoming emotional, take five long, smooth, rhythmic, deep breaths, and repeat relaxing words to yourself, such as "calm" or "self-control." As you take slower, deeper breaths, you'll feel less anxious and more in control.

15

STREETWISE STRATEGY #7: ALWAYS PLAY FAIR

I believe in fate, but at the same time my heart doesn't accept its randomness. Our relationship with the Universe is not passive. Every ounce of our wit, energy, and intelligence has to be applied to improve the hand we've been dealt. And without fail, we must always—always—play fair.

Burrel

The other day I saw a popular celebrity in downtown L.A. I was leaving a restaurant and he exited behind me, entourage in tow. Outside was a cluster of kids waiting for a sighting, a word, or, if they really hit pay dirt, an autograph. But this guy wasn't having any of that. He breezed by, leaving only fresh air and disappointed faces in his wake.

Though the incident didn't even cause Mr. Celebrity to break stride, it sure gave me pause. You see, I know this guy, and I know, too, that when he was coming up through the ranks, struggling and battling to break through, he'd have been beside himself with delight to see kids lining up for his autograph. Heck, he was so thirsty for attention back then, he'd have paid money for kids to mob him! So how is it that he suddenly has amnesia? After all, it's these same kids, or kids just like them, who put him where he is today. Funny how folks forget that, isn't it? Funny that they forget who was there for them when they needed it. Funny that they forget to reach back after they make it.

Funny that they forget *the little guy.*

Every day I watch people scrambling over one another to climb up some kind of socially defined "success" ladder. No matter how unstable or rickety that ladder might be, they dedicate their lives to climbing it. And then, when they get to what they think is the top (because, of course, there really is no top), having stomped on hands, heads, and hearts to get there, they must channel all their energy into staying up there.

Hanging on to that ladder with both hands, they don't have one free hand to stretch to anyone else, to reach down to the guys whose shoulders they stood on. Or perhaps they're up so high, they don't even see the ground anymore. They make the mistake of forgetting that whatever goes up can, and usually does, come crashing down again!

LEAD WITH INTEGRITY

Without a rich heart, wealth is an ugly beggar.

Ralph Waldo Emerson,
Writer and Philosopher

It's probably never been tougher to recall the value of integrity than today. Look at the ugly diet of "entertainment" dished out on reality TV, where lying, betrayal, sneakiness, and cheatin' seem to be rewarded every time. Are these new human behaviors? Of course not. But they sure look ugly when you see 'em up close and personal on TV.

Why do people behave so badly on TV? I call these people, with their desire to grab a little fame before they disappear into obscurity, *the minnows.* They are not necessarily small in stature, but they definitely have shrunken in heart, spirit, common sense, and potential. They are rarely real players—and never Giants. They're D-listers on track to being Z-listers, grabbin' at the straws of fame along the way.

Seems that with this new celebration of bad behavior, there's not much room left for honesty, generosity, and fairness. Given all the garbage spewed out by the media, it's no surprise that we become emotionally calloused, and think it's okay to behave as badly as these people do. I can see why folks make the mistake of thinking the ruthless, single-minded pursuit of fame is a reflection of life in today's "me-first" world. After all, they call it reality TV, don't they? Too many people think that kind of behavior is appropriate for the office, the basketball court, the nightclub, or even their relationship—any place there's competition. They think that winning, no matter the price, is the only thing that matters.

Show class, have pride, and display character.
If you do, winning takes care of itself.

Paul "Bear" Bryant,
Legendary College Football Coach

Look, I'm sure as heck no saint, and I've served up some pretty bad behavior that is way more *reality TV* than anything you'll see on the small screen! I like climbing success ladders, too, but today I climb using optimism and aspiration, and I *don't* stomp on fingers along the way.

> *Real integrity is doing the right thing, knowing that nobody's going to know whether you did it or not.*
>
> **Oprah Winfrey,**
> **Media Mogul**

I've discovered one of the most rewarding things in life is the enormous satisfaction of bringing others along with you, and in recognizing that the people who were there for you in the beginning are the ones you want with you at the finish line. At the end of the day, life may not always play fair, but *you* must.

> *If there is anything I would like to be remembered for, it is that I helped people understand that leadership is helping other people grow and succeed. To repeat myself, leadership is not just about you. It's about them.*
>
> **Jack Welch,**
> **CEO of General Electric**

WHAT PRICE WINNING?

A life isn't significant except
for its impact on other lives.

Jackie Robinson,
First Professional African-American Baseball Player

Remember, when you place winning, or personal glory, ahead of everything else, you may pay a higher price than you can afford.

I read a news story about a young mountain climber, a guy named David Sharp, who died on May 15, 2006. I wrote about him in *The Burrel Report,* my regular newsletter. David was on his way down from the top of Mount Everest when he died. And he died after dozens of people walked right past him, unwilling to stop their own climb to the summit to help him. Now, of course, these folks had paid a great deal of money to get to the top of Everest, and we all know that it's every man for himself up there, don't we? So heck, why should they let a dying man slow them down, or stop them from "winning" the ultimate prize?

So here's a question for you: if getting to the top of a big hill is the ultimate prize, then surely your competition is a combination of the physical elements and your own human limitations? Agree? So if you were to push yourself to extraordinary mental and physical achievement, beyond anything you had dreamed you could do, and beat the elements, too, while saving a man's life, wouldn't this be a *far* greater victory—one with a real prize at the end—than some photo opportunity on the top of a big hill?

Apparently not.

David Sharp's death was followed by a global *excuse-fest*: "The guy was too far gone," some of the other climbers cried in defense. "Nothing we could do! After all, what would have been the point in risking ourselves for someone who was already lost?"

Interestingly, when an online poll by MSNBC (total responses: 11,565) asked the question: "Would you abandon your ascent of

Mount Everest to save another climber?"—the vast majority of people put humanity above "winning":

Yes: 96.0%
No: 3.8%

Sadly, for David Sharp, 100 percent of respondents who passed him by that day, as he lay dying near the peak of Mount Everest, clearly answered: "no."

My point? It's all too easy to *win the game* and *lose the championship.* I wonder if those guys who got to the top of Everest will ever be able to look at their snapshots, waving a flag from the roof of the world, without thinking about the dead eyes and freezing body of the guy they passed along the way?

In my experience, winning for the sake of winning is *never* worth it.

A few days after David died, another climber was saved by a climbing team, which stopped just short of the summit to do so. Exhausted and freezing, they gave up their own glory to save this man's life. Their guide, Mazur, had no regrets: "Oh, yeah, it was worth it," he said, shortly after the rescue. "You can always go back to the summit, but you only have one life to live. If we had left the man to die, that would have always been on my mind. How could you live with yourself?"

Even if you'll never get closer to a glacier than eating a Popsicle, it's worth asking yourself this: "Am I the kind of person who'd reach back or walk on by?" If your answer is "reach back," then how about starting today? You don't need to be on top of a mountain to be there for someone who needs you.

Never worry about numbers.
Help one person at a time, and always start
with the person nearest you.

Mother Teresa,
Famous Humanitarian

FAIRNESS IS A BOTTOM-LINE DECISION, TOO

> *You have not lived today until you have done something for someone who can never repay you.*
>
> **John Bunyan,**
> **Author**

Never confuse fairness with weakness:

- Admitting to being *wrong* isn't weakness, but strength.

- Giving *credit* where it's due is a smart investment in loyalty.

- Recognizing and rewarding results is the best way to generate even *better* results.

- *Giving back* is a powerful demonstration of success and strength.

Famous billionaire Warren Buffet has given away billions of dollars to philanthropy. Not only that, he's insisted that it all be spent in a specified time, so it can be used effectively, today, when it's needed so badly. Anyone mistake him for a soft touch? Didn't think so.

> *It's easy to make a buck.*
> *It's a lot tougher to make a difference.*
>
> **Tom Brokaw,**
> **Anchor of NBC News**

Let's talk a little about loyalty. In the commercial world, companies pay a fortune for loyalty. You see, they know that when you invest in building relationships, you are really investing in something called *lifetime value*. In other words, those customers who trust and like you will come back, again and again, to do business with you. In fact, a customer's lifetime value may generate ten or even one hundred times more *return* than the initial transaction.

Now I could spend a lot of time talking about the business

implications of this, but I want to focus on the human equation. Think about the amount of investment in time, talk, effort, and emotion that goes into creating the best friendships, the best partnerships, or the best marriages.

Now think about what happens when you stop making that investment and simply allow things to drift. Look how trust unravels, ties loosen, and folks simply float away. When you allow this to happen, you've wasted your total investment. Think of it a different way: imagine spending millions of dollars on building a beautiful home, and the day you get the key to the front door, you turn around and walk away from it. What a waste that would be!

It's no different when it comes to building relationships. You've got to put in the *investment* if you want a return—whether in terms of love, friendship, or loyalty. So when I talk about *playin' fair,* what I'm really talking about is doin' right by the folks around you, and the people you touch every day, year after year. In short, each day should be infused with respect and consideration for the next man.

A while back, I watched a program on the Discovery Channel (man, I just love Discovery Channel, don't you?) about two guys whose character and courage were tested in the face of overwhelming challenges. I must admit that the end of the program left me with more questions than answers, and made me take a long hard look at myself.

REAL TALK
Climbers and close friends Jim Sweeney and Dave Nyman are scaling a sheer ice-wall in the shadow of Mount Johnson in Alaska when Jim falls and is badly injured. Dave initially leaves Jim under cover, heading to the nearest ski lodge. He arrives exhausted and stressed out, after traveling for miles across inhospitable and potentially lethal glacier terrain, but is incredibly relieved to find some skiers there. No one has a radio, though, and a search party sent out to find Jim returns empty-handed. Dave feels he has no

choice but to head back up the mountain to find his friend.

In the meantime, a passing light aircraft sees Dave's improvised SOS signal carved out of the snow in front of the ski lodge and tries to land, but in doing so, damages its landing gear. On board, the pilot and his injured pregnant wife—seven months along—are now stranded in the icy wasteland, too, as bad weather closes in.

REAL TALK

Could it get more complicated than that?

Yup. Amazingly, Dave finds his friend Jim, where he left him, buried in snow, and over the next few nights, the two survive a number of brutal avalanches, are swept down the mountain twice, and, finally, after getting caught up in a third avalanche, tumble into a deep, icy ravine.

I'll explain what happens in a minute, but at this point I have to tell you, I was doing some soul searching.

First of all, if I were Dave, would I have gone back to find Jim? After all, I'd done my part. I'd hiked for miles and found help. If I went back up that hill, odds are I would never come down again.

Second, once back up on the freezing mountain and unable to get Jim down, would I have stayed by his side?

Through night after night of near death experiences, Dave stayed by Jim's side, dug the incapacitated man out of potential snow graves, built shelters, and tried to keep him safe from the elements. A losing battle, as it turned out.

But the third question is maybe even more difficult to answer. If I were *Jim*, would I have demanded that Dave stay with me (which is what Jim *did* do, by the way), even knowing my best friend would probably die with me? Does any friend have the right to ask that much?

So what happened?

Well, through almost superhuman feats of strength and bravery, Dave achieved the impossible. He dug a path through miles and miles of snow, dragging Jim behind him, inch by inch by inch, until after seventeen hours, he collapsed in total and complete exhaustion. Even then, there was no rest for the weary. After yet another avalanche hit them, and hurtled them into that deep ravine, Dave located Jim, dragged him up a 70-degree incline to escape their icy tomb, and then continued on down the glacier. Eventually, they were spotted by a small plane, and everyone was rescued.

Now Jim might argue that asking Dave to stay was the right thing to do. After all, he had faith in Dave; he knew that Dave had it in him to save them both, that there was never any doubt that they would both survive. Jim might also argue that loyalty counts above all else, and it was Dave's *responsibility* to stay. But I tell you what, I find that line of thinking hard to swallow. There's no doubt Jim's selfishness came close to costing Dave his life.

Dave, on the other hand, admits to some "dark thoughts" as he wrestled with resentment and the urge to save himself. However, once he finally decided to stay, he felt vastly relieved ("Debate over!").

Sometimes these ethical questions are the hardest of all to answer, because there really is no right or wrong. Even though I have no doubt you would *never, ever,* find me at the top of a glacier (I'm a city boy through and through!), if for some bizarre reason you did, I honestly don't know how I would have acted. I'm a courageous man, but also highly pragmatic. After all, I'm a graduate from the streets with finely developed survival instincts. I have a feeling those survival instincts would have kicked in big time. On the other hand, I'm deeply loyal. Loyalty to me is *priceless* and *powerful.* When I am loyal to someone, I'm committed. I'd like to think I would have put my own interests second, but let's hope I never have to find out.

WHAT GOES AROUND . . .

The game of life is a game of boomerangs.
Our thoughts, deeds, and words return to us
sooner or later with astounding accuracy.

Florence Scovel Shinn,
Self-Help Book Pioneer

He probably saw the young kid in the wing mirror before he heard the shots. We'll never know for certain, but Wiz wasn't the kind of guy who missed much, so my money says that he saw it all unfold. I imagine his gaze colliding for a split second with that of his would-be assassin and, in that bitter moment, seeing the stark, bleak reality of his own death—and life. He took two shots to the head, blood and brains splattering the dashboard of his beautiful new car. He died instantly. Wenny was thirty years old.

My good friend Keke and I paid for his funeral. I grieved for Wenny, but I guess that's how it goes down. I've seen too much that appears to be so inherently unfair that sometimes it's hard to believe life isn't just a roll of the dice.

There's the good guy who loses his woman to a cheating, violent asshole. Or the guy who gets fifteen for burglary, while the cold-blooded murderer wriggles through the net.

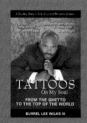

I've seen guys killed because they left the house five minutes early, or five minutes late, or because someone with a gun was in a bad mood that night. I've seen guys shot in cases of mistaken identity, boys who are dead or crippled because they were in the wrong place at the wrong time and caught a ricochet. Then again, I've seen a man survive with thirteen bullets pumped *point blank* into his body.

I believe in fate, but at the same time, my heart doesn't accept its randomness. Our relationship with the Universe is not passive. Every ounce of wit, energy, and intelligence we have has to be applied to improve the hand we've been dealt, and without fail, we must always—always—play fair.

In all the years I knew him, Wenny *never* played fair. His hand needn't have been a losing one, but he ensured it was. In the end, there was certain tragic symmetry between the way he lived and the manner in which he died.—From *Tattoos on My Soul*

Live as if you were to die tomorrow.
Learn as if you were to live forever.

Mahatma Gandhi,
Spiritual Leader and Pioneer in Civil Disobedience

YA GOTTA DO IT

ALWAYS PLAY FAIR

Don't know how to start making a difference? Making a small effort, every day, to do one thing that benefits someone other than you makes all the difference in the world. Pick up the phone, make a call, put in a word for someone; take a moment to have a genuine chat with the quiet guy in the next office; volunteer to help out a friend, a stranger, or a cause you believe in. Reach out, reach down, reach back, and, above all, be the kind of person who is known for always playing fair.

To laugh often and much;
to win the respect of intelligent people
and the affection of children;
to earn the appreciation of honest
critics and endure the betrayal
of false friends;
to appreciate beauty;
to find the best in others;
to leave the world a bit better, whether
by a healthy child, a garden patch, or a
redeemed social condition;
to know even one life has breathed
easier because you have lived.
This is to have succeeded.

Ralph Waldo Emerson,
Writer and Philosopher

INDEX

INDEX

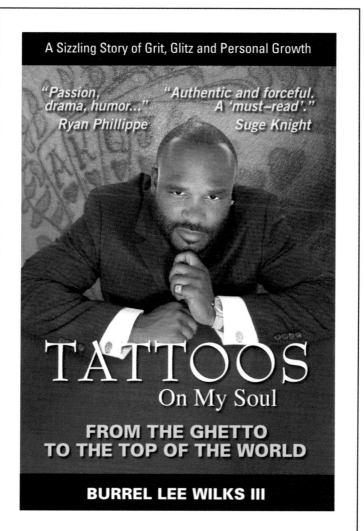

A Sizzling Story of Grit, Glitz and Personal Growth

"Passion, drama, humor..."
Ryan Phillippe

"Authentic and forceful. A 'must–read'."
Suge Knight

TATTOOS
On My Soul

FROM THE GHETTO TO THE TOP OF THE WORLD

BURREL LEE WILKS III

For details on where to buy a copy of Burrel's memoirs, check out www.tattoosonmysoul.com or www.ipgbook.com